W9-BZV-911

I travel

in *rusting*

burned-out

SEDANS

A life inside poetry

Melissa,
keep up
the great work

JIM BOHEN

Jim Bohen

Copyright © James E. Bohen 2018.
All rights reserved.

No part of this book may be reproduced in any form whatsoever
without the written consent of Unsolicited Press (except for brief
quotations in critical articles or reviews and in non-commercial
uses permitted by copyright law).

Cover and interior design by Samuel Merritt
Author photo by Brian George
Author's website: https://jimbohen.weebly.com

ISBN: 978-1-947021-24-2

Library of Congress Cataloging-in-Publication Data:

Names: Bohen, Jim, author.
Titles: I travel in rusting burned-out sedans: A life inside poetry /
Jim Bohen.
Description: First Edition, Unsolicited Press [2018].
Identifiers: LCCN 2018933969 / ISBN 9781947021242
Subjects: Poetry, American.
LC record available at: https://lccn.loc.gov/2018933969

Published by Unsolicited Press
www.unsolicitedpress.com
700 SW 5th Avenue
Portland, OR 97204
(619) 354-8005
Unsolicited Press books are distributed to the trade by Ingram.
Attention schools and businesses: Discount copies are available
for bulk orders. Please contact our team at
info@unsolicitedpress.com.

for Bonnie

Contents

At the Corner of Lyric & Strange

I travel in rusting burned-out sedans

Rants, Laments, Sermons & Smiles

Final Movement: Mostly Darker Notes

At the Corner
of Lyric & Strange

quiet

quiet as starlings walking on grass
is the no train whistle not yet
calling, the no combustion not yet
whirring, the no drive whine not yet
screeching or squealing today —
all while the no rain,
holding off its wet and falling,
remains content with rations of gray.

and quiet as the no train not yet
rolling is the no abusing, the no berating,
and the no reproaching —
while the not yet weeping no fall rain
is waiting to approach the ground
and loosen the hold of
a not yet scolded dressing-down.

and silent, as leaves postpone release
and delay descending, is the driving wheel,
content to hold on tight to its not expending,
content not to cough or roll or move,
not to pull, push off or run away,
content not to offend the no
sound that it knows will
end, sooner or later,
some time
today.

First Thunder

Pacing in neutral *got old.*
The waiting-room paper,
walling off spring with steroids
on dull, was driving your distraction
to a brassy breaking point.
So you unpeeled

like an onion, bounced off echoes,
scratched to places where you
wouldn't be subject to any sudden
laws involving jarring

decibels. Next you must choose:
Jet roar? Mumble?
Ruction? Dust-up?
Harley stutter? Roller coaster?
Dodge-'em cars?
Rock-the-skies-up, baby,

with a no-jazz-spoken-here,
that-was-a-helluva-bang
we heard? Then it's on to where
you next announce
your next-to-us report:

CRaaAAACK, surprising —

rippling,

fade.

Mirror Man

The mirror man woke up
this morning to roll himself up
like an old program
so he couldn't see
the grass that grew in
his feet, the stars embedded in
the small of his back. When he's
out walking streets, he knows
that frames ache
for him, spray-guns itch
for him, drip-rooms wait
for him, their lead needles

twitching, clenching, on edge.
Mosaics want to collect his hard-backed
bits, so the mirror man loads up
his devils like buzzing bee-bullets,
folds himself up in secretive
moons that move like
the mouths of unschooled fish,

and waits out of sight —

but not out of mind.

He is blowtorch glass sucking in sun,
spewing razor-light forth in
the late afternoons when the moon
hasn't started its cursory run,
hasn't thought through

what needs to be done.
The glass-blower's
waiting in the glass-blower's room
to take him in, to make him be born,
but the mirror man hides from

the hammer, cocked,
the drip-torch, on.

The brush, in the glue-pot,
patient, composed, expects one thing:

to wait him out.

Flying Near Dawn

The explosions flicker,
then the amber-lit city winks
out . . . and is gone.

We are flying from the long night;
we are flying near dawn.

A mist ghosts alive,
attacks with a rip a fabric of clouds;
it wants to slice up their canvas
to wrap up some bones
but then the mist, too . . . is gone.

Blue shades begin to arc above a dumb
white grin; fingers of frozen
lava separate snow into islands and deltas.
Rose and orange hover above a carpet
cloud. The clock decides
to move and we are flying near dawn.

When the unfocused impressionistic
sky deposits us back on the ground,
we walk out of our dreams
into normal and hassle,
fumble and grief, the gray
of the now and the drag of again
and the grinding out of another day —

a day that may find us rooting
for dreams, any dreams

still flying near dawn.

Accident

Runway grass blowing
in streams. Tiny marking flags
rippling straight in jagged

salutes. The TV and the internet,
the everywhere-you-turn
chatter . . . daggers.

Tears and wailing
in a concourse,
at a briefing,
in the morning,
in a week,

in a year.

Runway grass growing,
flags pointing,

photos in frames.

The Beyond

the beyond after you stop calling
is black cloud mornings,
dirty ice, dusty roads
ungone down,
shanked and pricked in
ungod's brown,
is gray. is gray

is night, is storms bending
through a prison yard,
is men who say their stories out,
pass-through-quick-then-gone-no-trace,
spill their guts out on the ground
without a hope they might be saved,
might ever get to even think of leaving

this place behind. the beyond
after you stop calling
is gaping, open;
is men beyond their ends,
beyond their wounds;
is women wailing,

silently;

crying — but not openly

— invisible,

betrayed.

Reluctance to Share the Night

The clouds permit their passing
gate to briefly lift its arm,
but it's only done reluctantly;

the wind has to insist, overriding
their resistance with
an electronic wand. Working
stars, scuffing past, in formations
they know well, slog their way
through clearing smoke —

then stretch to fill
the bluest rooms with a thoroughly
counterfeit glow. The clouds
are bothered, definitely,
but there's nothing they can do.

All the stars have hit their marks,
not one has missed a cue.

Tell

A tell in cards. A telltale sign.
But is there a tell when you phone
it in? Or is it just a tale told
by an idiot, signifying nothing
in the telling once it's told

or on a cell?
When you tell William Tell
da-da-dot, da-da-dot, da-da-dot-dot-dot
or to go tell it on the mountain,
be sure to tell it like it is.

And when you tell someone a thing or two,
be sure to embellish with each re-telling.

When you get your 15 minutes of fame
(to tell off or to try to shame),
are we talking show and tell

or simply someone else to blame?
No way to tell?
If you tell tall tales, tell tales
out of school, or pen a telling tell-all,
is it tell-on-you time, tattle-tale,

or is it all just very telling?
Tell the truth and shame the devil.
Tell the truth, the whole truth
and nothing but the truth, so help you,

teleprompting television.
Tellers may be disappearing —
not so kiss and tell. Do tell?
Oh, please, please, pleeeeease:

doooooo tell.

I went to the water

I went to the water breaking
the legs of the crickets' songs.
I went to the water, shoving, grieving.

I am the angel, with black wings, tiding.
I am the six-legs, rubbing my eyes
in the dung-town and rising, numbers
of millions of dark
afternoons. I am creeping
ice-hearts that somehow do not

melt away. I am the fan-ax,
flailing inside secret rooms.
I am not at all the sequential
moon but the chrysalis in need
of asylum, a need that only brings
a far that masquerades as something
soon. For the black-legged forager is
out, looking for insanity,
not to cool me off but to make me
glow more — so I will engulf

the room. I am hanging on water,
on its every word,
on its syllables and cadences,
on its tongues and its absurd.
So I can't hear you, haven't seen your
vain attempt to copy what I do, am not always

rubbing my eyes awaiting your approach.
When I am a great beast, shoulder to the stone,
trunk pushing over trees, peeling
off cricket songs, stripping off black wings,
orange wings, striped wings, strong,
I am sitting in the dung pile making sandbox

cities rise and I haven't time for you.
You wouldn't either if you could see yourself
as I have seen you: coming to water, rubbing
your eyes, shoving, grieving,
weeping.

The woman walked through the door

and into paradise, where archangels
and seraphim rang out hosannas
and golden crowns gleamed in an ecstatically light
and rays and glitter, sparks and praise came showering
down upon a vast and thunderous applauding assembly
and the scene fades slowly to black,
silence buried in ringing ears . . .

Draggy shoulders droop through rooms
stacked with soap and wax. Shuffling feet
insinuate a carpet into dust. The cupboards
speak a musty tongue,
thin and dry, an unknown language:
slowly tick and slowly tock,
tick - tock   slow - ly.

The door leads into a world
of shopping bags and repair receipts,
spring lilies and the rose of
deceit, dripping drip drop, drip drop.

And the seraphim sing on Friday nights
down the street at the neighborhood
bar, each hosanna spoon-fed whiskey
slurring one more blistered
tongue residing in a desert place
where lizards aren't the only ones
who still know how
to tongue and run.

Psalm 148 Revisited

Praise the heavens, the sun, the moon,
praise all the stars that shine, give

praise, for the universe is a mighty creation,
a miracle of colorings,
a magnitude astonishing,
a feint, a map, a sleight, a bluff,
a wile, a chart, a diagram that every
one should marvel at and wonder at
and try to figure out, especially

those who thought they once
inhabited its core, were the one and lonely
beat that pulsed inside its only heart.

Praise be to a universe of elegance,
of violence, of mysteries.
Praise be to its artifice and camouflage we

do not fully grasp as yet,
likely will not ever
fully know.

Birds, Rising

on the lake the white bird rustles,
leaving scars behind in black.
the other birds upon the water,
startled from their mostly slack,
are now alert, now apprehensive.
with lifted necks, they're watchful,
waiting, craning for a midnight wind.

moving with the first breath blowing,
sensing it was time to leave,
they wrestle with the water mother
who cradles them and tries so hard
to rock their other soul to sleep.

but then, majestic, white swan rises,
sisters, brothers, sons and daughters,
trailing, tracking, following.

rocking from their leaving waves,
the water tries to call, cannot.
it forms a message, cannot speak it,
knows the sad that's coming on.

they are leaving is the message.
they are leaving, leave us weeping;
they are leaving, they are gone.

Northern Heat

Hot up here always comes
with a stucco of sweat
that wants to pant
but doesn't know how.

Prairies sulk. The moon
would rear and wander
off. Can't.

Salt-drained bones.
The curve of the wind
duning the night. Chalky

sheets cannot hold —
not even a pose —
and cannot learn to tame
desires. Even when flames

that refuse to be washed
no longer snap and roll.

Small Talk

Laying in for Winter

Tell me a story, any story,
so I have something to pocket,
something to pull out one dark
day, the kind when you clean
out every nook, every place,
then look for more, to find
something — anything —
you can use.

Now Finally Arrives

If I ever thought of now,
it was always a place I'd never reach.
And if I did, it would certainly see
others in boxes,
others in urns.
Not me.
I'd never reach this now from then.
But recently, I spotted it —
now, that is. It was rolling into
my station — and it was
right on time.

Windmills

look like giants
flailing their arms in a modern dance
that doesn't involve rhythm or feet.
They listen for a screeching train,
braking hard by moonlight,
bearing witness that any blue hours
or memory day
may be nothing at all.

Life, Unexamined

Omens. Shadows. Blades.
This does not bode well, not at all —
too dry, today. Too fly away, tomorrow;
too pulling up a blanket on one fall
out of blue, one never-seem-to-care,
one walking-right-on-through.

It's like living without ever
thinking of water, without ever
wanting to know if true —

is wet.

Winter Garden

Snow stacks up where lilies, bee balm,
iris grew. Yellow, orange, purple, peach
have all surrendered, white flags
raised, sticking through the snow.

But there is a tinge of, trace of, hint of
not-giving-you-the-satisfaction
of a subtlety of blue.

Cold Wind

The wind's rough hands flick
at our borders, shrinking what didn't find
somewhere to hide. The wind does not sing,
by the way. It can't, though wishes were
tokens and there was a slot to put them in.
Listen. You can almost hear them —
easy, rolling down.

Boards Hard Used

Boards hard used by wind and sun,
longing for paint, get gall instead,
look like cheekbone skulls on dread —
except without the white.

Wait a minute, start again —
boards hard used are not like skulls;

all they know that's pushing dead
is gray.

Memories

Alphabets of light remain —
a fermentation congregation
tending toward a spray of rain
that wants to dream of sun,

that's drifting with wind
that won't delay, cannot stay,
has to run.

Tumbleweed

The wind can blow you free,
but it won't provide
for morning — any type,
any style.

What happens after waking up?
Always up to you.

The This and That Poem

This poem starts this way.
That poem heads in a different direction.

The two barely acknowledge each other,
and, when they do, it's a not-on-cable didn't
happen couldn't have event.

This poem commits to elite, you see, is prepared
to fight off anyone who couldn't possibly fathom
its depths, couldn't possibly understand what's buried
in its difficult, multi-layered and/or
surreal text, what's salted through
a suite of poems on serious mythic stuff.

That poem is approachable, conversational, trying
to make a friend, though a lack of social graces
and far too few connections may doom it
to fumble its only real chance.

This poem uses metaphor, symbolism, heft.
It may seem disconnected, and may, in fact, not know
its why, its core, its beating heart —
but it's really really heavy, really really
educated, really really smart.

That poem might consider taking a tepid
chance — but only very briefly.

This poem flaunts its references, may wear
a coat of academic dust.
That poem could care the hell less.

The two eye each other warily, like circling
knights enacting a clanking bravado. They worry that
their heavy armor might cause them to trip
and fall — should they ever decide to cease their operatic thunder,
stop their rattle, threaten to call a bluff.

This poem worries that it might be a grandiose
but empty shell. That poem wonders:
was there more I might have taken on?

Both poems follow a path to . . . well, to what?
Enlightenment? A sigh? A collective
gasp or laugh at a sparsely attended reading?

Both poems have access to scoff, but it's also
true that this poem — and that one as well — secretly fear they're
not in the know, that
something is lacking, that others, who snicker,
may see right through their latest clothes

and hang out with the real poems.

Vacant

Barefoot on cold tile.

Lounging in long rooms
with cigarettes,
imported beer,
a sudden sense
of doom.

Fires are waiting;
sod soaked full.

Warning

they edge our years in
sullen, stain our
lives in pocket grays. we always
underestimate how well they know
what they need us to do.
if we forget, they have ways

to remind us. they heap it up,
they break it down,
they turn up from somewhere beyond
some mostly uncharted sea
with the hook of a con of an ecstasy,
with a sweet-talking promise
of better days when all we will ever want
to do is do things just their way —

do *not* believe them.

they want to pump our hearts
white and go; they want to slough
their disdain on us, want to wield
their nameless breaking things
from behind their friendly smiling
masks till we choose to sleep
under tight control. their control.

you would be better off in a cage
with a hundred hungry tigers;
you would be safer if the only food
to offer them was brass and gold
for a thousand million years.

Lanterns

When bodies —
standing by walls,
strolling in streets,
stooping under
the weight
of stairs — are

vaporized
in an instant, do final
thoughts escape? Do
they have time to float
on winds or whisper
a forget-me-not in
someone's ear? Perhaps

they take their final ride
in lanterns, softly lit,
in lanterns, floating off,
in lanterns, bobbing
quietly on waters
drifting off somewhere
to gone and maybe true . . .

away from life
and out of time,
away from
any vision,
away from
any view.

Coal Man and Harlequin, Dancing for Tips

why do you write poems like this,
gleaming of coal-stars, indignation,
crowing of victories you never won?
why do I always see you reaching,
the people filing out the door,
you still preaching as you slump on a filthy floor?
why do you sit there alone with a bottle,
alone with your papers,
your fear and your twaddle?

I tell you, have patience — we'll get there yet.

the coal man led his devil on stage
on a long choke-chain,
the harlequin head flopping and dangled.
the coal man lit his red-striped soul on fire
with a grimy seduction,
his grease-paint exploding into silver chips
the stagehands will pick up later
when it's time to go home
and feed the kids, pay the babysitter,
and peel back the covers till next
day comes and the owl is sleeping it off.
turns out they'll never find what exploded
so they hide and shriek about losing
some sleep. the manager's coming; he's got
the hook that ends all the clatter, ends
the contract scratched in before.
it's time for dread, totem carved —
it's down in the book in crooked letters.

why do you write these?
I must make a dollar.
why do you write these?
I haven't a cent.

27

once I danced on platform shoes,
was never gray, no feet that ached,
but now I am split between two worlds —
I think I will hear the owl soon.

darkness, and I am holding hands up to my ears
for I fear the owl has been silently
screeching, only been toying and playing with me.
I grope in the wet field and scramble for cover,
I'm watching my breath as it melts away.

why do you write these? look what they lead to.
fuck yourself over and leave me alone.

the owl sharpens its talons
in crisp gold bark;
crumb-dust gold flakes down.
the owl could have stayed perfectly still —
talons won't be needed today.

I travel in rusting

burned-out sedans

First Day of School

Scary tremendous number of faces.
A room he's never seen before.
First day at any school — missed the first week,
sick. He holds his mother's hand, peeking
from behind a pleat. She reassures him one last time,
drops his lifeline, backs away.
Her face and waving fingers slip into
the crack of the slowly closing classroom door.

The nun's very large rosary, hanging on the belt
of her habit, clicks as she leans down. Her face,
ovaled in black and a stiff white bib, smells like soap.
She shepherds him a few steps closer to all the kids,
arrayed on the floor in front of him by the dozens.
They're kneeling on haunches, sprawling
on elbows, sitting, yoga-style. The nun may speak
in a motherly tone, but the words of comfort
don't register — at all.

The nun smiles.
The kids, squirming all over the place, don't.

As she introduces him to the staring eyes,
he can't find a single boy wearing shorts.
He is wearing shorts, is more anxious than he
was before. Wherever he looks, eyes on him
seem to try to burrow in, seem to want to get inside.

He looks at his shoes, at the teacher,
out the huge bank of windows
where the sun streams in.
He sweeps the room: neighbor girl?
The one who lives next door? He can't find her.
He is alone. He fidgets, stares at the floor.

They all know.

But he doesn't cry —

he has been five for seven whole days.

Playing Pirate

My uncle Larry, still hugging his kid at age 16,
commandeered a stepladder to make
an assault on a pirate ship. When he fell off
the ladder, he gored his thigh
on the thick wooden point of our
white picket fence. The blood pulsed.

I remember his groaning and yelling and crying.
I remember seeing his legs convulse
on our bathroom floor.
My dad held him down so a neighbor nurse,
who'd raced from right across the street,
could work to stem the bleeding
and prevent his descent into shock.

My mother, anxious about her youngest brother
but very much collected, too, gently shooed me:
Play outside. I was seven.

I remember dried blood on the picket's point.
I remember the ladder, lying at an angle,
the loser in its tangle with the fence.
It's been 60 years but

I can still remember —

and every time I do I wince.

500

After some swings and misses, a foul pop or two and some
weak-ass grounders — and more than a few complaints — the kid
finally connects, lifting a fly to waiting gloves. Camped under a
can of corn, you're ready to make an easy catch when
. . . the taller kid bumps you aside, makes the grab, snatches
the fat 100 points. He's well on his way to what's needed to win:
500.

Being smaller, your only chance to win the game (and earn the
right to hit) is to chase down every grounder, every hopper, every
roller that the big kids often disdain to pursue: *Why bend for a few
puny points unless you really have to?* is how their thinking goes. You
also need the taller kids to fight over flies and flub a few — errors
mean deducted points.

If you think about it, 500 offers some very good lessons. It's
good for your math skills, of course, because you need to track
each kid's account. The game also provides something of a lesson
in how life really works. That's why you don't complain too much
— as if you really had an option — because an older you will do
the bumping and the cutting in, the laughing at the "no fair"
whines and the thrown-down gloves as you hoard all the points
you want, which have a way, amazingly, of growing, sometimes
"magically." When you start to tire of the game, you may —
"may" being the operative word here — you may let a younger kid
win . . .

. . . but that only tends to happen when
        you reach a certain age

                and a magnanimous feeling
                rises in you —

                        as some girls are walking by.

33

Radio Scores

Giants-Dodgers, 1962. Pennant race.
The radio: the only way a Central time zone kid
who loves the Giants gets the scores
of late-night West Coast games.

So my boxy plastic white clock radio, on the floor
by my bed, is tuned to WCCO, a 50,000-watt,
clear-into-Canada local AM behemoth.

Not too loud, though — barely audible, in fact —
because I'm supposed to be asleep on a school night
and I don't want to wake Mom and Dad.
But with all the static, I sometimes have to
move the knob and the volume can shoot too high.
That brings Dad trooping up to my attic room.
The radio went off. Sometimes it stayed that way.
Not in September, '62.

With no play-by-play, all I had were occasional scores
read by the host of the late-night show,
Franklin Hobbs. You could tell he wasn't
a baseball fan. His show, "Hobbs' House,"
was on till the morning farm report. He played music I
had no interest in. His mellifluous voice —
there's no other word — could certainly put me to sleep
waiting forever for updated scores that seemed to take
for-*ever* to come. So sometimes, despite
my best efforts, the next thing I heard, with my alarm,
was the noisy annoying morning crew.

1-zip, 2-1, 1-1 tie — the scores rarely changed.
No surprise there: Koufax-Marichal,
Drysdale-Sanford. But when a Giants' Willie —
Mays or McCovey — or maybe Cepeda
or maybe Alou got a hold of one
(I found out who the next afternoon in

the now-defunct St. Paul Dispatch),
it was "yes" in a whisper. It was "yes" when
the Giants tied it up or took the lead, angst when
they lost it, fell behind or failed to erase a deficit.

The Giants took the prize that year, winning in
their last at-bat. But they lost the World Series
with the tying and winning runs in scoring position
in the bottom of the ninth in the seventh game.
It took 48 more years for them to finally win
the Series — something they chose to do, no doubt,
just for a Job like me. Now, when I can watch

the Giants anytime I want, it's hard to stay
awake at night to see the end of any game
that's playing on the coast.

Hitchhiking on a Country Road

The beasts approach, each answering
mad the call of the other.
Sometimes they couple
outside my universe, wild in the fog;

sometimes within.
The trees, the house, the nearby field
are all I can see, standing by the side
of this road among what must be setting stars
obscured by fog, lost in deep,
with the which way out
is home? — your guess is as good as mine.
When the beasts are gone,
I hear a bird calling,
a dog barking,
a road going.
There's a stone on the road spun up by a wheel
that detoured onto the gravel apron.
There's a mailbox and a telephone line
and a way —

                in   and   out.

I'm alone.

But it's morning yet, there's hope
for escape; let's hope it's not noon or too soon
it's night that finds me waiting,
stuck on still while beasts approach. A mist

slightly dampens the page where I start
to write this down. The bird calls its single
note, again and again. The dog barks
off and on, shoes pace the sand by the side
of the road. It's started

to rain. The doppler beasts return.
To them, I'm-gone-as-I'm-seen-as-I'm-gone.

To me, they come unknown
from outside my ring and leave the same.
They come with lidless eyes
and a whine that builds and grows;
they go out on a doppler tide,
receding, subdued, gaw-awne.

On My 22nd Birthday

Chalk-white skies, gray-toned.
It's still a late-in-summer day,
but cold awaits this Virgo's child.
Fall will send its wet wind
chill, then winter hide our
darker things from a spring it keeps

arm's distance off — for what will
seem a too long while.
Twenty-two years old today,
I sit at home, stare through glass
and think about what they want
me to learn: they want to teach

me how to kill. The sky is baffled.
The dusk seems slow to fall.
A puzzled winter brushes boots to prep
them for the snows to come.

All the seasons exert their pull
while I, twenty-two years old today,
recall that I once thought the stars
must surely know the force
that started driving them to burn
so very long ago.

The Ape

the nearly naked ape
squats briefly on the kitchen floor.
he rises to write formica
words he hopes — no, dreams —
that other apes will want to read.

but the cats know.
they smell the old game
as he writes on a grimy table,
pinching crumbs

with his pen.
they purr and cat-soft
lay out sleek, bellies stretched,
padded feet, *is it food?*
then purr some more and bleat
and crawl between his legs.

near the piled-high sink,
he's trying hard to make sure of
it all with bicarbonate of soda
and by keeping watch so

the soup won't burn.
he does all that as screeching
tires send a knife right through
his brain — his viperish, serpentine,

get-by brain.
and a bottomless cave
that has wanted to form

begins to open inside his heart.

The Locusts

for Sylvia Plath

the locusts have been here,
eating my stomach, picking my brain.
they left the chewed cobs of my mind
thudding together. hung in
the whip-wind with stalk-whip
handles, they're humming, buzzing,
brazen. when the cobs are dull, they fall,
littering fields, only good
for silage and mice.
the farm family living there must nibble
their hands, must wring out
their sweat and save it till spring —

it's all they will have to eat.

it is green and weeping here,
it is summer turning fall turning winter.
it is you, dead these years,
reaching back tendril hands;
it is you, reaching back to pull
me into your world sooner, to lull
me with words you borrowed
from death that I don't want, that you
should have given back.

leave . . . no, stay . . .
no, leave, please leave.
I am only a red mouth in a bad month sometimes.
I build my tunnels free of moles and marrow.
my mother is not tonguing me, licking my fur.
I lay no eggs, dripping yolk on cardboard sand.
you cannot have me. I will not go.
I will not be pushed by you

or pulled by you,
cajoled, seduced or prodded by you —
I just don't have it in me.

sometimes, I admit, I devour stray
hooks and spit them back transformed,
but not as my father.
I only make small packages,
deliver smaller squeaks. too much
sucking wastes me. my walls
may bleed a bit sometimes
and sometimes the crows look ready
to peck my eyes out —
and sometimes maybe I wish they would —
but I am different than you.
I want to live, I want to survive
(though let's set aside
the why for now, that's something
for some other time).

I know that when the locusts have been here,
feasting on my fat grain and sucking out
my sweet juice, I might not notice
that your hands are mist and cannot grip,
that your belts are thin and cannot hold me
down to be dissected;
that your wings are not saws
that can prune and rip;
that your mouth can't do its jagged thing,
can't make incisions, sever, cleave;
that your tongue no longer sucks
that hard, that your teeth no longer
cut and tear as they might have done before.

I don't need you.
I already have the locusts,

carving me up,
stringing me out,
gutting me,
piece by piece.

Rock Band Days

1. The First Night I Ever Sang in a Band

I had diarrhea so bad that day
I was, shall we say,
a little raw.
Thank God for Vaseline.
It was May 7, 1972, and
I figured I'd have a chance
to watch the Lakers try to win the title
on my breaks that night.
But the bar had no TV.

A total of 15 people
saw my debut, and five
were regulars who only ducked
their heads around a corner between
sips of beer and 8-ball shots
to quench their curiosity
about what in the hell the racket
was they were forced to listen to.
We were only paid a fourth

of what the owner promised (final tally:
two bucks each) but, to make up for it, he gave
us a huge American garrison flag. He didn't
want it because it only had 48 stars —

and it was dirty. Well, the Lakers won the title
and I didn't get to see it — after waiting
to do just that through a string of
almosts stretching back years.

The band lasted for a while, though it was
nothing special. The flag?
It covered a wall in our practice room,
though a dog had done its duty — from
fading stripe to faded star to very plain-to-see.

2. *Lead Singer*

With the driver lines and the lead wires hot,
the beast beneath the earth
leads me in to take my place
to be strung out once again.
The beast is cracking houses, breaking waves,
convincing fires that they are not yet
hot enough to heat the space.
I am singing on the wires.
They vibrate and quiver. I gyrate and crawl.
I prate. I prance.

I must be dreaming.

But if I did not sing,
the driver lines and the lead wires hot
could not fulfill their duty stringing
out from me — and the singing wires
could not ring and the sullen beast
could not be seen to bend his grace notes,
heat his pitch or turn his key . . .

. . . so he could sing his song through me.

And if I did not dream it all
or carry the beast upon my back,
you would still be keeping score,
still be wishing ghosts

like me would dangle
just above the floor,
strung with lines and burned by lights,
so you could see a high-wire act —
red hot, white hot, more.

3. After the Gig

Early morning's best — stars up,
two-lane winding home. Smoky
windows, wine-night air. After a quick
rehash, some jokes, it's wheels just rolling

back the miles. If it's road-song, snake-night,
flashing trees, then it's no-jive pick-ups wailing
lowdown blues nohow. If it's pin-prick lights
in dark instead of won't-win small electric vocals,
then all the dials are switched to off, the moan
put back inside its box. Nearly home,

we coast. When we're called, we'll step back on —
we're owed a brief encore.

4. *The Band Almost Breaks Up Again*

After screaming heavy chords for nickels and drinks
in a grainy club with walls that would have
trouble thinking they were even tacky, we were back
where we started, ready to roll another way.

Back home, there would be time to soothe
a raspy throat with honey lemon tea. But now,
after saying things we shouldn't, we huddled
in our headlights' world, the focus on not
over-driving our lit-up cocoon. Trailing behind,
our instruments of deafening praise, our tie-in
to the circling stars, lay stacked, silent . . . ready.

Rain would have completed the scene;
it didn't rain.

We plowed home, piled into our tired and cold,
ready to start again, ready to start it all over again,
ready to aim for the next time we would hook
up to the clear night fall of boogie rain
and rock it as far as we could go.

5. The Band Breaks Up

water drips from a faucet
in the next room. we

talk. paper is
shuffled. a chair
creaks, then
creaks some more. we

talk more and, yes, agree,
but then we undecide —
before we do it all again and

do it even more. and where
have we been in a year

is asked. what will

tomorrow bring is helped
by a breeze

from the west. clouds,
strolling past, reveal

the moon.

Sex

zig-zag volts
      halts and
            jolts no exes no ohs no ones and through

episiot my crescent moon

      place braid our fingers cut them

                loose to moan with thighs

i will not unravel you cannot unmake
      me you cannot get behind my
         mask or open me up to get

                  inside my velvet
     doors or shut

        me up from singing about
          obsessing about

            the hollow
               chamber

                   missing
                    bullet

want some don't
       it's lonesome here inside

    these blues

The Mississippi River, Seen from
a Moving Car on a January Morning on
the East River Road in St. Paul, Minnesota,
North of the Lake Street Bridge

The fog hovers
on the half-frozen river
like intermittent smoke on a now
silent battlefield.

The trees on the retreating
banks hold up their arms
without complaint.
Like prisoners waiting for orders
to march somewhere,
they're relieved they've survived
the carnage for now.

The scene is what bone-cold
feels like in a winter kind
of country when you wake up tired
and your too-old car
has trouble getting warm;

it's what bone-cold
feels like when you're approaching
the tunnel of another long
slog of another long day
whose slow-motion arrow —
just launched from the bow —
is not coming back again.

My Bachelor Great Uncle Frank's Tuxedos

must have sparkled in the 1920s,
ballrooms expecting them, dances demanding
their fashion, their presence. The tuxes must have
showed just how they felt in a bold art deco
zigzag world — as they flowed around
the satin floors and saxophone women stroked
the walls sporting geometric forms.

When the tuxedos came to me, I tried on every pair.
Nothing fit. Over-padded shoulders. Baggy pants,
too short. Suspenders. They were clown suits.

Then, ah, then, they were dashing and handsome —
oh, how he must have pulled her in tight
to the strains of white jazz and the tipple
of bootleg bathtub gin. But then my uncle lost
his hair — it all fell out on his pillow one night.

So he shined the pants on banquet chairs
and left his tuxedos, preserved
from every kind of moth, to me in his will.

It was only a week or so after we moved
that I finally remembered I'd left them behind.
They were hung in the closet of the empty room where
we'd kept our mad cat jailed for a week —
before we decided we had no choice but to take him

in to be put down.

Evening News

a small light appeared
behind the newscaster
on the map
of Vietnam
to show the place
where the bombs
had dropped that day.

when the light flashed on,
my nephew, only
two years old, pointed
quick, said *Oh, star!*
and smiled at me.

Sharp Toys

I retreat into our friendship
with circled arms, soft words.
I throw madness through
the broken screens,
give it back to a screaming world
that wants to play with sharp toys,
that believes in detonation.

We light our own spark
and carry it slowly in our hands
so it won't go out. It flickers,
but burns. We may want to crush
it out at times, but we hold off,
we calm down, make it glow instead.
We place it on our altar,
make it our only sacrament,
build it from our need.
We take it down some nights
and blow and rub and sweat
till it gleams.

When we awake, we put it back
inside our consecrated place
until the next time
mad worlds, old griefs, sharp toys,
make us take it out again,
brush it off, make it glow.

I can see her growing old

I can see her growing old,
can see where the lines
will drill in deep.

I can even see where
the new ones will form,
where the skin will spread,
where the corners
of eyes and mouth will
droop, puff, sag, creep.

While I sit here writing this,
she's asleep —
very much a beauty to me.

When what I foresee finally
comes true, I have this hope:

that I'll be there
to enjoy the view.

Thoughts While — and After — Half-Falling to the Ground from the Top of a Step Ladder Two Stories Up

I can't believe this is happening!
I'm certain to stop on the porch roof, right?!
Nooooooooo!

After I hit the ground, feet first —
I'd maneuvered with all the control that I had
so I'd miss the sidewalk and roll on the grass —
I laid back a moment and pondered a bit on
how far I'd dropped in so short a time.
Feeling foolish as grade school kids —
there were hundreds right across the street —
pointed at me and snickered, no doubt at
the loud "woe-oh" I'd voiced
as I half-jumped off the roof, I had no choice
but to tell the tale more than once.

That's because my sister, who happened to be
waiting in a car to pick up her kids, had
just happened to see the whole thing as she
just happened to glance in her rearview mirror.

This makes me wonder the following two things:
First — was this incident a proof that God exists?

And second — this is undoubtedly a family story
I will *never* hear the end of —
especially now that I've written it down.

The Clouds

Having started, reluctantly leaving,
I am rolling on a prairie in a car
between destinations.
Bored to arrive anywhere, I start to deceive
myself with clouds, the giant balloons
waiting up there for Macy's Thanksgiving parade.

Like blown-up bubbles, they take many shapes,
but only the large ones make my list.
Dragons; airplanes (with propellers); giant mice; geese
with their long straight necks roped front, pulling sleds,
their wings paused for another downward thrust; star
ships; pig snouts; railroad cars in line; giant hands,
palms up, holding cotton, making secret signs.

Why do I list them? I ask myself.
What is this need?
Why another traveling poem,
another catalog, another dream?

What is this <u>for</u> *?*

The kids, sitting in back, plugged into music or video
games, already too old for clouds, quickly lose interest
in playing my game. My wife, who's driving, has more
basic things to attend to. Only I can hover, waiting
with clouds over prairie. But waiting for what?
For the image to change? A song to resume?
For questions to answer themselves?

And why do I list the things I imagined —
exactly as seen, no changes at all?
I could list whatever I want to later — but I don't.
And why note that the clouds I saw seemed to be
resting on some kind of table, their bottoms sheared
flat by some kind of saw, some sky-slicing saw

that might have ripped through, methodically,
carefully, hours before we'd even set out?
I have no answers to all these questions
but I am able to tell you this:

The last clouds I saw were puffed-up
sprinters straining to hear some starter's gun —
placed on a shelf by someone or something
eager to see who would win, how they'd run.
Focused intently on the first pylon,
they dreamed of breaking a glorious distant
victory tape. Indifferent to all but the race,
they were between their destinations,
always starting, almost leaving.

The road curved; we angled with it,
approaching a different
metaphor. Still not arriving, I
also wasn't deceiving myself
with clouds of any kind or
sort, blankly bobbing,
quietly weaving,
blowing slowly
away, strings
still stretch-
ing long
and out,
trying
soooooo
hard to
stay
taut.

The Ground War Begins

It is night on this side of the world.
A sickle moon and a few stars
pierce the dark. A powdery snow
buried us under winter again today.

The stillness is only broken by wind
chimes telling a secret somewhere
nearby and by the muffle of jets
hauling weary people off who've
earned some r & r. Small white clouds
of flak glide past. My shovel
disinters brittle brown leaves
left behind from the fall
and tosses them up onto snow berms
with the latest troop of crystal soldiers
who floated down to lie in state today.

Cars sleep in their bunkers,
dreaming of conceiving at the pump.
The rutted alley awaits the plow
and the shrieks and moans
of its scraping bayonet. Snow dives
off railings, looking for cover in
trenches. The wind chimes keep
tolling their random tune. And
the summer's weeds, long laid to rest,
are deep-sixed by an ocean of white
that encoffins our litter
and entombs us in a pretty shell.

Except for my breath,
there is an awful stillness.
I lug my weapon on my shoulder
and, as I trudge back to my home base,
I march my boots to Sunday
and a dream of June.

The Trip

The whale hills breach
their scarred white humps
from deep inside the Wisconsin
prairie, pointing stillborn
cilia at a bleak gray sky
imparting its wisdom in rain and sleet . . .

that will turn to snow later tonight,
with possible blowing and drifting tomorrow
and into the weekend for sure.

A young woman sings
on the radio (does so very achingly);
a semi, mounted upside-down on a very large
roadside pole, promotes a local business;
a crow wheels away from a thermal
pull; a tunnel mutes some wind.

The whale hills mole slowly
through sod, arched backs fading, receding,
away. Their tails, swaying, undulating —
are flicking, rucking, teasing, gone.

Our daughter's college adventure begins.
The projectile rolls through
the grayness to some sort of destination,
knowing nothing is ever resolved.

The Artwork

for Richard Brewer

I decide not to stoop to read the name
of my friend's piece of back-drilled art.
The framed and painted plexiglass stares at
me from low on a wall at a gallery show.
I check out the work's main shape. Is it

a Cheshire cat's grin? Intelligent, devious,
playful? Ready to unleash some sort of
mischief at the slightest provocation before
slinking into shadows to smirk, or scampering
off to enjoy a howl, to paste a cackle onto its wild?

Or

are the crosshatch etchings inside curved
intersecting lips part of a gaping
maw? Am I looking at rows of razor
teeth ready to grind whatever appears,
whatever ventures in their path? Is this a trap
indifferent to suffering,
to any cries for mercy or reprieve?
Does its impassive look, its neither
smile nor scowl, mean that it can never touch
a trace of sad or glad, that it can't think or feel
at all? And does that mean, as it marches on,
forward and inexorably, that all it is

is a neutral   clockwork   eating   machine?

That's quite a few questions you've been asked.
But rest assured this isn't a test —

Or is it?

Keeping the Kids' Stuff

How long do you keep the kids' stuff
after they've moved for good, the Barbies
and the other toys, the files in plastic boxes,
all the grade-school art? Do the
board games go, nestled on a basement shelf
your thirty-something son "forgot"?
The toy guns in the attic, now politically incorrect?
And what do you do with the projects?
The ones that got an A were all you chose to keep,
plus the ones the teachers must have
somehow just flat-out misjudged.
And what about castles and what about cars,
or the over-muscled action figures
somehow not called dolls?

You have the space. And you don't have to dust —
and *won't* — won't chat aside the spider webs
with a *Why do we keep this stuff?*

There's always *Save them for the grandkids.*
If you're lucky, that's an hour — one day tops,
at best — before screens entice their fingers
to a dance and dance and dance.
What other use for opposable thumbs?

So in the end, easy choice, the stuff can stay —
for now. Not ready yet, no, not yet time.
And when it is, you can rest assured the job
might be a paying gig for some poor someone else.

All Her Things

preparing for the estate sale after Mom's death

We've spent days sorting and moving:
figurines, one-of-a-kind teacups,
trivets and jewelry, linens and books,
decorative tins, small wooden boxes,
wicker baskets, ornate frames, cut-glass bowls —
and Aunt Mari's porcelain, most of it glued
(to Mom's despair) after horseplay went too far.
From the tasteful to the tawdry,
the graceful to the garish, our sorting
and hauling draws smiles over here, yawns over
there, and some funny remarks — some perhaps
with a hint of a barb buried somewhere inside.
Finally, after days of shifting boxes and filling tables
with knick-knacks and stuff of every description,
the family has gathered inside the garage —
we need space to sort through Christmas.

Mom loved holidays, especially Christmas.
It gave her a chance to entertain
and buy everything all over again —
candlesticks, tablecloths, stuffed toys, trays,
napkin holders, glasses, towels, plates, even child-size
choirboys plucked from some department store.
She could amplify her gathering ways:
ornaments and villages, garlands and wreaths,
bows and twine. She could emphasize silver
and lather on gold, cater to glitter and glow and shine.

They were part of what made Christmas
magical for her and for us when we were kids.
So, when it came to Christmas, she probably
didn't have too much — but she certainly came
damn close. In the end, after all our work,
after all the sorting and moving, if we discovered

anything — besides the folly of too many things —
it might be this: Mom bought or acquired
every piece and admired it once, briefly or not.
She thought it had a place in her life, whether she used
it a little, a lot, or it ended up stuffed
in a closet, forgotten. At some point, she held each thing
in her hands, admired its shape, climbed into
its sheen, enjoyed its colors or how it felt, may have even attached
some dreams, whether any were there
or not. We did not share most of the moments
Mom had with her things — now in boxes too many,
on tables too cluttered, taken from walls once
far too full. But despite sore backs
and balky knees, we saw a bit of what she saw,
touched a bit of what she bought:
a cacophony of sparkle and brilliant and pearl,
a riot of color, the delicate piece.

I will never know exactly what space Mom's things filled
up for her, but I — we all — touched at least a part of it —
touched some part of Mom at least —
sorting through all her things.

The Intersection

A stream of hovering cottonwood seeds
rippling like milk along a curb.

A plastic bag — up back around down
inout   thisway   upagain   thatway —
a no-sound   slow   ballet.

A man holding a sign —
Homeless, any help welcome.
It's rush hour, busy intersection.

The brief stay in "poetry" clicks itself off.

I exchange nods with the man.
But I look away quickly, not wanting to give
a hint of a signal that he should approach.
I could afford to give him a little money
but I race through my checklist instead:

- It's-a-hassle-to-fumble-for-my-wallet;
- I'm-pretty-sure-I-have-no-ones;
- giving-change-is-too-cheap;
- there-isn't-time;
- maybe-he's-just-a-con-artist;
- giving-just-encourages-them;
- I-don't-want-to-inconvenience-
  the-line-of-drivers-behind-me.
- I-wonder-if-I-have-time-to-raise-
  my-window

if he crosses traffic to try for a touch?

My lack of generosity bothers me . . .
but he has money for his addiction
to cigarettes . . . though he also can't be
rich in much if this is how he stands a post.

The milky seeds, forgotten, are,
no doubt, blowing away.
The plastic bag, no doubt at all,
renews its dance.

The light   turns   green.
I escape — without delay.

Trial by Jury

Defendant. Finally on the stand.
Quickly in tears.
Then combative, guarded, evasive:
doesn't know this, never learned that,
doesn't know what that is.

Government witness. Plea agreement.
Swears that now it's just the truth,
the whole truth, nothing but.
Repenting now, he's seen the light;
knows that what he did was wrong — but
only after burying things,
only after he was caught,
only after jail was staring him smack in the face.

One lawyer plays with a rubber band.
Another one talks too fast.
Security guard may be nodding off.
Octogenarian judge, still sharp,
keeps things light but in control.

Boring repetition.
Jurors — who can't discuss the case,
who don't want to be there at all —
paste small-talk over all their divides,
bury their eyes and fingers in phones.

Justice? You hope so. It's your name
on the verdict form that's sending
grandma off to jail.

Late Fall Dreams

I

Spin on the front lawn. Dart, duck.
Drop back, stiff-arm the wind, the air.
Flip the ball ahead, then run under it. Get tripped
up for a first and goal as you make a sliding catch

just shy of the sidewalk end zone. Trot back
to the huddle, brushing off leaves. Breathe
that roar-of-the-crowd sound as loud as you can. Pace
back and forth, trying to remember more of
the names and what you want to happen next. Tick
off some statistics. Keep up the radio play-by-play.
It's the big game against Iowa for number one
in the nation and the hope of your state is blowing

its warm on your red and roughened cupped fall hands.
Get stuffed for no gain or a loss sometimes.
Let a pass hit the ground off straining fingertips.
Even lose a fumble or throw an interception.
And punt? No choice, because third-down
punts were commonly used when field position
was hoarded like gold.

II

When he watches games on TV now,
sitting in his bathrobe
in a wheelchair in his crowded single room,
he scoffs:
*This isn't football — it's fast-break
basketball on artificial turf.*
He spits out *artificial,* lands
harder still on *turf.*

When he stares out the window, I know
exactly where he's gone,
exactly how crisp the fall air feels

when it rustles leaves and tackles boys
to a cold and damp
spin-to-winter waiting ground.

Bionic Man

Hearing aids with chime-playing anti-tinnitus programs.
Numerous fillings, crowns.
Missing teeth. Discolored teeth. Crooked teeth.
Two front teeth pulled because they were rotting from
the inside in a process called resorption.
A thigh that goes numb or tingles from meralgia paresthetica.
(The same thing on your back: notalgia paresthetica.)
Restless limb syndrome, also known as Willis-Ekbom Disease.
A medical brigade of pills — for this, that,
the other, the next. And then there are the eyes —
the whole thing done in miniature.

Flashers. Floaters. Specks. Astigmatism.
Chalazia. Crow's feet. Drooping lids.
One eyeball a lot longer than the other.
Strabismus, causing double vision, a.k.a.
diplopia. Severe myopia. 20/so-many-hundred-something vision
that my eyes are almost off
the chart, which is, by the way, a blur.
A corneal problem with the name
map-dot-fingerprint dystrophy — unless you prefer to call it
anterior basement membrane dystrophy
or Cogan's or its other name.

And the latest: acrylic foldable intraocular lens implants
with UV blue light filters. They come with their very own
ID cards so even my wallet gets fatter. Cataracts gone,
but I still wear progressive bifocals warped by
something called prism. And the posterior capsular opacification
in my oculis sinister (clouding in my left eye) needed a Zeiss
yttrium aluminum garnet laser
to blast a hole in the center of my lens
capsule with mini plasma explosions in what is called
a capsulotomy. And, after all that,
my eyes, or my eyelids to be more precise,
can turn playful when I go to bed. Nerves

firing like tiny tripwires slowly trek across a lid,
seeming to say: just try to go to sleep.

All this is just the prelude to the bionic man's shopping list:
shoulder surgery, replacement knee, corneal transplant,
more pills, plastic surgery for
sagging eyebrows in a vain attempt at vanity,
a stent or two, a pacemaker, more pills, a walker,
a wheelchair. Add bridges and fillings that start
broadcasting messages from aliens
and I'll start to resemble a Borg — and I'm not referring
to the Swedish tennis player.

Sounds like a bright future . . . if I'm able to hear it, or if
some new dystrophy — or the aliens —
leave me enough teeth so I don't have
to gum my bloody baby food.

Cold Snap

I

To get out of the cold, we quicken steps.
But that's just an illusion — trust me.
Inside our boxes, heat and light
do the dragging, the pulling,
the shuffling around —
we just follow where they lead.

II

Less to see, less is new.
The world thinks
it's inventing things —
all the time, something new.

We know better.

Wasn't that a style not all that long ago?
A version of it, anyway?

Doesn't he sound like . . .?

Everything old is new again,
one of us may say.

Is it really that long?

Nods and silence.
Facial muscles barely move
enough to form a smile.

III

The moon, which ever makes
its rounds — bound by gravitation,
sweeping space without a sound —
and showing still, brightly down,
the same face it has always aimed,
is pointing to a pile
of shirts waiting for a drawer.

If its light could reach the closet,
it would smile on stacks of blankets.
They are waiting, patiently —
on their shelf, in the dark —
hoping for a gentle shake,
a warmly spreading out . . .

. . . or a leaving home for somewhere
    else to do their job again.

My Favorite Coffee Cup

It's ugly. It's *really* ugly.
Bulbous shape.
Horizontal circling stripes.
Clashing colors.
Large dark red stripe, two thin ones
mingle with pastel blue, brown, yellow,
cream. When you don't like pastels —
and I don't because they're washed out
and creepy like Uriah Heep —
you're usually looking at ugly.

I only like the cup because it's larger
than average, so I need to fill it less often.
I guess it's more of a mug than a cup
but, whatever it is, it's ugly. Its
homely deal is clinched for me when you
throw in its throw-up drab green stripes:
old-fashioned institutional trying
to lead a parade.

If the cup survives unbroken,
it will huddle in a garage-sale box
or head for a Goodwill store someday.
I hope it breaks before that day because I
wouldn't want to know whoever might be
tempted to buy it, no matter how cheap
the price, or — God forbid —
walk off with it for nothing at all,
a bargain to be carefully cradled home.

Falling

Fall, not spring anymore.
Not even summer.

Space concentrated; ephemera
melting away — unless they're needed
to waste some time, to forget where
the months refused to stop
to look for a place to try to kneel
to approximate what we call pray.

Fall, *not* autumn.
Shivers loom.
Houses and all manner of things will
drape stalactites, crack with ice. Elements
of doom-clocks will — if they sound
— not be heard.

Fall . . . later.
Can you answer:
Have you done what you set for yourself?
Will you try the sums again
you couldn't do, gave up on then?
The sums you thought you'd never want
to ever come back to?

Late fall, winter soon.
Birds, with names you never
even bothered to try to learn, flicker for spaces
at a feeder out a window after snowfall
blanks the all around.

Absence of color.
Engines make the only sounds.
Shades becoming visible.
Stars move to the edge of town.

fall.

feeling small . . . very small.

Discovering an Old Man Living in My Mirror

I always had my suspicions but the face
in the mirror was always a blur when I didn't
have my glasses on. And since that accounts for
decades of blurs, I never could prove he was there.
But now, with both of my cataracts gone,
I can finally see who I missed. I'd like to go

back to before. My eyes may have looked like
pins back then, when seen through my old lenses,
but their thickness covered some aging sins. Now
I've detected some stranger residing inside my mirror:
he's some old man who seems to be there

with all his Dorian Grays revealed. His face has
small lumps here and there. Discolorations, lines
of all sorts. Hairs where they shouldn't be able
to grow. Large age spots on the sides by his ears
that I think I only glimpsed before. Jangled,
weedy brows. A scraggly beard less full
than I thought. And a small white circle under an eye,
reminding me — don't ask me how —

of Jupiter's great stormy spot. So — as I finally
face the facts about who I hadn't reflected on —
do I have some sort of mortality phrase —
my "to be or not to be,"
my "for whom the bell tolls" —
that I can offer you? No, I do not.
No such memorable phrase. But I can add this:

My eyes, seen again at their full size,
are all that remains of the acned youth
who braced his smile with tinseled teeth,
who barely had a hint of the mask
that he would wear, stare at so clearly
so late in the year.

Latest Attraction

for Hazel Charlotte Bohen George

When your first cry leaps
from your just-has-to-be a beautiful face,
gift shop shelves will set toys free and
miracles alert the press that they will be passed
around. Church bells, forced to ring, won't

dare indulge in a case of will not. The snow
will hold off one full year; the birds not
navigate south from here. Salt will cut back its
negatives; spice hold its heaviest fire.
And the stars? They'll begin to up their game.
See me, they'll say. *No, me. No, me.*
No, me, they'll say, raising their hands like

frantic kids, like people who signal
a rescue plane. The winds will start to lower
their game to the level of lovely breeze, setting
the stage for a perfectly beautiful, gorgeously
wonderful, marvelous no-fuss day. Clocks,
on schedule to hold some ticks, must give us
an hour or two for free. Traffic jams must

melt away, distribute their cars to the poor.
Why all this hyperbole?
Any museum's must-have piece —
a living, breathing sculptural prize —
will have finally safely arrived!

The northern lights — jealous, churlish,
out of sorts — will put on subdued, low-key
shows before a quick retreat.
What else can they do?
More would be unseemly, would be showing off
and they know it. National holidays

will grow by one. Fireworks will
flower and fly. And when she barely opens

her eyes, even though she can't see much,
the world will not be tired, climate change
will take a break and missiles will be set
to off, the children wrapped in target rings
winning an all too brief reprieve.

Oh that she could keep it that way
when she's old enough to really sing.

Rowing for Real

While rowing toward some awful god,
a civil war rocked my boat.
Sparks ricocheted off mast and wheel,
working toward amok.

But it was all a tease.
Only I was there.
That other me, the not-myself?
Found a way to hitch a ride so I
wouldn't dwell on alone so much.

It's time to stop the trifles we use
to plague our rowing, stroke our minor
key of blues. Time to row the frenzy
stream, find the island of that god,
drink its acid, bang out its song,
plug some sockets deep in its ground
to search for, find and suck its fire,
putting up with paltry burns,
sirens that may wander by —

especially when we start to sense
the fire might not last the night
and we don't know what still remains
of what we need to learn.

I travel in rusting burned-out sedans

I travel in rusting burned-out sedans
with suicide doors, dirty cams.

I always seem to bring too much
of the wrong along.

I catch things that I cannot name,
should not try to hunt or seek.

I eat wishes, which is why I'm always hungry.

I rest on downed trees, sit backed up to bark
that scratches at complacency.

I sleep on easy if I find it, hard if I don't.

I'm troubled that my choices aren't really
mine to make.

I am haunted by water, flowing or frozen.

I hope what's in dreams isn't there in awake.
I wake to a hope I forget what I dream.

I want to learn if hope is real.

If I cut my arms to hide things there,
I want them to clot, scab, heal;
I want them to peel, bleed . . . care.

I hack at tendrils grabbing at eyes, *my* eyes.
I limp from torches. Cut by claws —
frantic, terrored — I'm breathing hard.

I travel in rusting burned-out sedans.

I am haunted by water, patient . . . waiting.

Love Poem

Somewhere I have never traveled,
far beyond the places where I have been or yet
may see, would I go to find a love like yours,
a love that nature stops to witness jealously.
There's sorrow enough in the world, sorrow
enough for the nevermore we all must taste.
So it can wait, can hide itself behind
your smiles that seem to banish every tear.

In your land, where dewdrops turning stars
can dance upon the slightest wind and slip
inside a feathered fall from heaven's store
of grace, you beckon flowers from the rain
and falling down to stars you make them shine.
(Your love can even make me write lines that —
any other time — would surely make me frown.)

Someday, I hope I'll make a place,
beyond abyss and fear, make a home with eyes
whose love will more than mirror mine.
For there, with nature stopped in awe of one
more love like yours, would I gladly make my life
and know no rage nor fear of death and never
think to go away before the light is gone.

Rants, Laments, Sermons & Smiles

the poems in this section work best when read aloud —

with a little frenzy . . . or a touch of resigned.

Game

I show horses, golden horses.
I hold sunshine. I smile lambs.
You be the oars of a Roman slave ship.
You be savage, Thracian, Goth,
in stinking furs and winter — waiting.

I am wander. I am leisure.
I pick flowers, taking my time.
You be the stray dog, no hair, licking.
You be the Jew in the Warsaw ghetto.
You be on the losing side,
bodies hung, bodies burned.

I am the lover on the far hills, dreaming.
I am the bride, smiling, laughing.
You be the target in a Japanese garden.
You be the fire in Dresden raging.
You be napalm, Vietnam, China.
You be sleeping long at Pearl.
You be the child, hungry, lost,
crying, cold and traumatized,
wandering streets of strange alone.

I am learning. I am knowledge.
I'm the stone lion guarding the gate.

You be Job on the dung-hill, weeping.
You be Tiresias, blind and lame.

Blues Rant

It is all sorrow, partings, endings,
shutting up shutters, closing up houses,
taking our leave. It is all, all of it, already past —
all gone, all dust, all end.

You know it.
Deep down it is inscribed
in your soul in a script
that cannot be altered or scraped away.
It is a furious pull we push against,
a tide, a weight, a rock, a fall.
It is Sisyphus on his hill, Atlas with his globe.
It is inventing God and religion,
fashioning empires from human hides,
holding onto petty jealousies as if they were gold.
It is people at parties trolling for laughs,
the telescope pointing out edges in time
as if any of it meant anything.

It is holding on till the final howling at
the final moon,
all sorrow, all sadness, all endings, all tears.

The moon will break apart,
bird songs will be silenced, green and sun
and stars will melt and fade and burn away.
The race is temporary, the day is transitory,
the dam   will   break.

We are steeped in denial.
We carry it, care for it, nurture it,
as if it were a cherished pot
that harbors char from many fires —
but the rusted wheel instead will roll
with a sorrowful weight it knows too well.

We make prayers, paintings, books, revolts.
We keep lists, have sex, celebrate, cry.
We kid ourselves, mock ourselves,
rail at our stupidity, injustice and hypocrisy
and it's all of a piece that's a sham that's a lie;
we agree to each bit till the wind dies away,
completely gone slack,
till death us do part.

The leaves will not rustle;
the grass will not grow;
the oceans   will   not   roll.
We create some Dickinsons, Shakespeares
and Twains, Mozarts and Beatles
and rap and jazz, markets and history
and cities and trends.
We fabricate numbers, TV, clones,
rockets, bombs, sex toys, drones;
football and farming and missiles and moans,
so much that's crazy, so much absurd.
Add a pinch of folly, grate in a leaf of pride,
powder up some greed and
granulate some snobbery —
then all that's left is stew and stir
and hope you have a place to hide.

We spit and gouge and fight and scream,
we backstab and betray,
commit honor and cowardice,
sacrifice and fanaticism,
love, devotion, tenderness, courage,
pettiness, bigotry, slavery, bondage,
faith, hope and charity — and denial.
Most of us cocoon it in to go along, to get along
because we're waiting for the moment,
the hour, the day when it's revealed,

when we will finally understand,
when the only question that must have an answer

gets one.

But there is no answer.

The temple is mute, the altar empty,
the wine in the chalice calcified.
The devil has locked us up and in,
the key lives on a hook on a wall
just outside our desperate reach,
just outside our lonely cells.
The answer isn't coming, can't be known,
does not exist, though we call and call
and call some more and gesture
with our bitter fists.

The drums fade as the troops march
over the hill. The cauldron sends up its last
prayerful of hopeful steam.
The book lies open, its pages blow in an empty
breeze while the tolling stops and stops till then,
then stops some more and stops again.

All is sorrow, all is endings, all will be over,
is over, has died, is buried,
has been forgotten, long forgotten — is still denied.
You know it. I know it. We all know it.
All that is left are parades starting out,
concluded before they've even begun
so the broom can do all its sweeping up,
so the tick tock that we're racing past
can try to do its hiding from

all is sadness, sorrow, endings,

all is leavings, dying dust.

Yet even I prepare for a future that won't arrive,
that's already past, that's already
gone, that isn't coming for me at all.
Even I still shepherd a brake against
discomfort, try to slow a stark old age.
Even I want my children doing well,
cooing babies to have their smiles,
that all will be happy, so that someday —
if trumpets or something should sound
from the sky — something of me will be there,
will be glad at least that all of us
made it to an appointed day.

It should be quite clear to everyone here
that I resent the hell out of where
we have been boxed:
in a plight we didn't make,
in a bind we cannot shake,
in a puzzle made from ache.
It is clear that I resent the hell out of
all is sorrow, sadness, leavings,
all is endings, dying dust.

So is there anything left to say?
Any relevant "takeaway"?
Going on seems the only one —
along with my apology for intruding

on our denial. So please let me wipe the slate
as clean as I can make it now:
I apologize   to you   for bringing all this up.

Poets on Sex

Brilliant coupling metaphors.
Towering similes.
Penetrating rhythms.
Erotic words hammered home.
Fingers caressing bodies to bliss.
And every climax coming hard
before the passionate symphony
ends on a very spiritual point.

But it does make you wonder.
Do the poets who write like this
do so from great experience?
Or is it just that they
want us to think that they do?

A murder of crows

The sounds resonate and soar:
a parliament of owls, a building of rooks,
a convocation of eagles, an exaltation of larks.

But why so many flocks and schools,
arcs and prides for birds and other animals,
but not so much for other things?
Why not a ring of echoes, a knocking of nails,
a celestial of harps, a wagging of tails?

Why not something to match the song
of a pity of doves, an unkindness of ravens,
a murder of crows or a scold of jays?

Ah, I see the problem. Soon language would
fill with a somber of sad, a screech of wails.
Do we really want a surplus of sorrows,
really crave a civil of wars? And do we want
those humming a dirge of denies
the freedom to write out a dictate of thoughts,
a command of requires, a descent of new sins?
Do we want a muddle of messengers?
Aren't there already people enough
nailing their meanings of theses up to their
mandates of closing more and more doors?

There could, of course, be a siren of songs,
a puzzle of poems, a tempting of rhymes,
because what we have is poetry —
a murmuration of starlings,
a lamentation of swans.

But these phrases lead, inevitably,
to an envy of smiles and a slaughter of sons,
to a gather of graves, a denial of daughters,
to a laughter of tears and an end of worlds.

Prison Gate

I slide, leisurely — there's plenty of time.
I shut with a satisfying, clinching sound.
Heavy. Locked. Final. Tight.
It's doing my duty, fulfilling my function,
reverberating properly along the thickset walls.
It's not my place to know if someone here
does not belong, so when the hours
are long and the smell of sweat will always
come from just one sex, you get
your satisfaction any way you can.

So young. When did they get so young?
And why do they still short their
lives so casually? Three here, five there —
the dance card's quickly filled.
Don't they see that schedule will

tattoo inside their brains? Some things never
change. They still think they're tough —
not what their hands are telling me. Move
as much as me — clutch for years and years
and years with my anchor locking half —
that's tough that means. Not the sour
tough of dreams that rocks away the hours
in self-defeating cells whose only songs

are in the key of blue. *Do the time.*
It doesn't mean at all what they seem
to want to think it means. I'd
shiver, but I'm made of steel,
so I can't feel at all.

Bitching

I bitch —
they die.
I kvetch that life isn't fair in a country
where war can be fought elsewhere
but want is still allowed.

I bitch —
though I'm not so poor I ration my meds,
though I'm not so poor I'm forced
to live where dumb luck
death occurs on a whim you
can carve in your schedule well in advance.
I bitch, though I'm not followed by security
guards, pulled over by cops,
even shot down inside my car or on the street
for committing the crime
of being black.
I bitch, though I don't have to ride
on an overloaded boat or train,
dig where the earth will cave, try to survive
by making beds, bleaching people's
vomit and blood, cleaning people's shit;
living by a no-tree hill that slides
down death when it rains too much.

So what right do I have to bitch at all?
I'm white, I'm male. I have most of what I think
I want, far more than many who dot
this rock have ever had or ever will.

I have *every* right.
Precisely because they can't afford meds,
are forced to live just where they do,
precisely because they have to die because
an asshole thinks they're a threat
or it's some revealed-in-stone god's will,

or precisely because some jerk,
who sees the earth as a giant pie,
wants a bigger, sweeter slice to boost
an ego, fill a void, wallow in a narcissist's high.

I bitch at selfish — including my own —
at greed and injustice, at things, at life.
I bitch and kvetch, complain and critique,
criticize, cry and bellow it out
with only a softening now-and-then note after
my rant runs out of steam
and a coo has replaced the retch in my throat.

I bitch —
they suffer and die, unjustly, sometimes horribly.
They die and suffer, again and again,
lives barely lived, some barely alive.
Me? I bitch. And it's something I will
continue to do until I'm unable to bitch anymore.

It's part of my job.
It's the very least I can fucking do.

Men with Loud Engines

Men who use loud engines,
engines that throb and cackle and buzz,
must have little . . .
Johnsons (unless they're using Evinrudes?),
must have little naughty bits that seem to say,
in decibels: *I'm cock of the walk; please notice
me and the size of the junk I wear each day.*

Men with loud engines are a little like . . .
- hairy organ grinders,
- family jewelers,
- peacocks with erected feathers,
- little boys thrusting swords straight up,
- trashmen holding their valuable junk,
- silly clowns juggling balls, or
- privates a bit crotchety that extra
  duties mean the end of hanging loose.

Men with loud engines must have a little . . .
need to connect with things that say wow,
must want to control the frightening forces
rocking us here and rolling us there,
that jazz us and jizz us and jerk us around.

Women using loud engines? No idea.
Get there faster? Be one of the boys?
Maybe these women are cat
lovers who just prefer their purring loud?

As for men with loud engines, engines
that rev and vroom and roar, these
men must be a little . . .
nuts (people who want to sleep will say),
must have little bones to prick with
a very scary universe that ignores
their little engines a lot
and treats them with a wan disdain.

Checkpoint

Thoughts denied entry at the border.

Words not welcome to combine as they want.

Songs censored — or cut at dress rehearsal.

Poems, dressed somewhat unfashionably,
discouraged from standing in receiving lines.

Books arrested before display,
before pity can even give them the chance
to live out their paltry ration of days inside
whatever is passing for print.

Pictures blocked, screens detained,
sculptures cropped, motion chained.

And gristled nights, trying to
insinuate the morning,
fail to shift any clock
toward the new or an old again,
fail to crawl inside reverse
or find a way to be escape.

Afghan Women Poets

The radio report said that many Afghan
women poets — not allowed to appear in public
by male relatives — must phone their poems in
to a meeting of their fellow female poets.
Most Afghan women poets use pen names
to avoid the stones and shards of a morality
that's good at flinging screaming pain,
indiscriminate bloody death.

American poets take their kids to soccer games,
birthday parties and the ice cream store.
We shop and socialize, free to write whatever
we want, wear something provocative,
complain loudly that life isn't fair.

Afghan women poets must decide whether
to leave their homes forever when threatened
by male elders for writing "immoral" poems.

Here, what poets write is free to be ignored —
as most poetry is. There?
No discussion. Death, just death.

One Afghan poet says she left her rural town
because she wants a life where she can
express herself. She's willing to die
a dignified death (which could be anything but)
rather than thumb herself under,
a life suppressed, a spirit caged, a voice denied.

Her courage makes me feel quite small,
makes me ask some questions:
Why do we let things like this happen?
Short of guns and bombs and boots
on the ground, can anything be done
to end things like this? How can people live

this way, denied what we consider a given,
a birthright almost as basic as breathing?
How can they live with death as
a next-door neighbor who can drop in for tea
at any time, then splatter the walls with
guts and brains? Because that's how it's
always been? Because there isn't any choice?

As inertia starts to regain control of
my fading-from-outrage brain,
the translation of a phrase one
Afghan woman poet wrote rattles my
detachment and reverberates inside my skull:

My country is burning; my heart is on fire.

Copper Faces

You couldn't have conceived of this
in any dream or ghost dance — your
photographs hung in a hallway
on the campus of a high-tech corporation.

But then the white man's ways
must have always been inexplicable to you.
How could they live, you must have wondered,
so removed from the earth, thinking that stones
and so much of creation are dead, thinking that
so many things should be moved elsewhere,
should be dug up, remade, discarded, destroyed?
Why did they think that so many people had to be
saved from their basic beliefs, had to forfeit
their language, their culture, their pride, their land?

Deer Running. Crow with Necklace.
Sarsi in the Algonquian Federation in Saskatchewan.
A Cree paddled a bark canoe while the Roaring '20s
flared and Henry Ford wandered like a ghost
through his River Rouge nightmare.

Assiniboin. Blood. Blackfoot.
Bear Bull. Calf Child. Come Singing.

Names like Soyaksin strained through
the net of another tongue. Full-blooded copper
not yet blended with the loud white tide,
preserved in photos so conquerors' kids
could enjoy what the sins of their forebears made —
in comfort, of course, with just a tinge,
though slight, of guilt — that good white
guilt we love to expose occasionally,
put on exhibit now and then.

The faces in the pictures make me pause.
If my face ever hung on some indifferent wall,
could it ever look back with dignity
in the face of so much sad?

Could my face ever be an echo —
unspeaking and dismissed —
of the prairie wind of white
that swept away the buffalo
and changed the face of God?

Pretty Moon

There's a pretty moon
at the turn of the stairs of my gone
youth, hanging in glass above a sill.
It's a crescent cup you can fill up tight
till the flow that goes down a long green
hill stops just short of a pretty windmill
with blades of blue and red and green,
bricks of sand and brown and white.

I can see my moon floating there still,
lighting the way at the turn of the stairs,
till I open my eyes to the real thing:
a rock in the breeze, a sudden
cold stone wading and creeping
through too many trees when the grass
is brown and the stairs
no longer know how to go down.

But my pretty moon, still there in dreams,
bears witness that everyone's
home from the fair with just enough
time to turn out the lights
and end the day with a quickly-to-sleep —

with my pretty moon still floating there
at the turn of the stairs of my gone youth,
in a dream of a scene that's etched
in glass that I have to, want to, need to keep.

Can't Make Them Stay

coffee skies.

— desert sorrows, sewn in pockets —

so they won't think to drag in dirt.

desperate migrants risking all

on so much deadly water.

OK, you've made a start to your poem.
Maybe done the easy part —
before the what-you-want-to-say clamors for a place.

But then some migrants interrupt, burst right in,
make their case. There's:

a trumpet blast

and   *shave the tower*

plus   *why can't time sometimes sideways?*

and   *why throb hum*

sky deep fly down?

How do any of these connect? What do you do with them?
Hovering out there, chattering on, coming close,
they tantalize, then skip off to a safe home base,
just out of reach, as if you're stuck in a children's game?

And what about the other migrants, trying to get their
tongues around the names of foreign streets?
Trying to make it around your town,
get past water, climb your wall?

burning air   wanders in — a little late.
         Do you let it stay?
                  And what about   *washing up on shore,*
                      the crossing
drowned them stone and dead?

Is there any part for these to play in
the what-you-want-to-say?

Damned if you know how they got in here,
or how you're going to make them fit.
Damned if you know what any of them
might think they really mean. The words you want
are washing away. You can't tag them, make them stay,
make them make some kind of sense that's
anything like what you want them to say.

So it's walk around in sorrow deserts,
skies of coffee tucked in pockets,
somehow dragging deadly water just above
the can't quite roll the words to stop,
the can't quite bring the words to ground . . .

to make them do what you want them to
after they're finally rescued from lost, forced
to hang around awhile, mixed without any
trace at all of strangers who made a run for it then —
but won't be smiling ever again.

Words like that are what you seek,
words that others might choose to pay
some of their store of attention to
if you ever knew what you wanted to say and
could make those words do something like that
today.

Barrio Shanty Ghetto Slum

Brother killing anti-brother; screamers scrubbing dark red dust
by blast by loud concussive too-tight quarters. No real streets —
garbage here, detritus there — repeated makeshift everywhere by
squatting shacks in full nowhere, repeating.
And we wonder why the lean-tos want the dream of living
just like us, who raise our windows casually that bar unwanted
bugs. Recycled danger, twisting metals in toxin brains, kids
kick a ball in unsightly pollution — we like to call it a drain.
The goal, a corrugated piece of roof someone once forgot
or took, will soon be remembered, retaken, reclaimed.
Heat, mad and spitting fangs, is never not there — except
on some of the winter nights when it would be welcomed
in. The dream is sidewalks, lawns, TVs, consoles picked
from console trees; toys, not-glued, remaining complete on happy,
gorgeous, dewy days. Scabby knees? Scrapey arms? Rounded
bellies? Stickly legs? Hazy eyes? Dirt for yards?
Out of view, not portrayed. Ads with unreal women, homes,
invade all of the too-dark eyes that blister into reverie,
finger-suck in hopefully. The foreign workers, trapped in
debt, must sell their souls or they can't leave, have the option:
hang themselves — which leads to more of gruel that
kids can boast they have achieved as they gorge on photon
fantasies, as much as they can, opulently.
The sub-drive acid protein strings, playing
angry music nights, stuck in bucket brownish sludge, don't
remind of pixeled towns, don't resemble pixeled skies that ripped
the colors off for good, leaving never-pixel dust, which wanders
where and when it wants,
smudged, dry, low, cussed.
Chemical dumps, booze, pills; black-market gas, work
the trash; slow-talk card games waiting to help the
pull-'em-up-go onto overload trucks, boats, trains; is it even worth
a what the fuck? It's satellite dishes siphoning games
in places that haven't the decency

    to up and fucking disappear.

They don't appear on any maps.

So what in the world are they waiting for?

What are they still doing where

pixels never come to dream?

A chatter of crows

We find so many ingenious
ways to waste our time.

But I was in luck when I looked up
from whatever was wasting mine,
because I saw
the chattering crows
suddenly flee from one big
tree for another quite nearby,

then squawk at their leader
(once they'd arrived)
that their newest latest haunt
wasn't any better
than the first had been.

America

A Poetic Hip Hop-ish Sermon/Montage

with Many Moons, a Dissenting Voice

1

I am in love with America,
with hands-up, don't-shoot, don't-happen-much-here denial, with
shake me, hip hop, so low to the bar
that king-me can reign all over our rights and hide
the intent in plain as plain sight.
Can you hear me now? Will you remember later?
Is there a product you will want that's better,
faster, greater than forming a union more
perfect from truths we hold self-evident?

Will your eyes still stare, your fingers fly? That's what we hold
most dear, of course, through the ramparts' most perilous fight.
That, and getting a nice free
lunch — paid for by people who don't have as much.

This is the start — what's intended to be — a poem on
                              America.
It will ramble, lose itself in gloom, tour through
a full regale of rooms in the land of the free and
the home of the brave where it's I want yours but lay off mine
in a zero-sum game too much of the time.

It stars a moon for the misbegotten, a second
chance moon, a half-blood moonscape — victimized,
possibly. It tolerates another voice while
barking at and howling at the shine on, harvest moon
for me, for me and my gal, America.

2

The flowers, balloons and cuddly bears pile up near
the stain; the ribbons tied to the chain link fence will soon be
frayed under spacious skies far from amber waves of grain.

O say can you see by the dawn's
early light what a polymer handgun sang last night?

That's such a cliche. Stop preaching to the choir.
Stop dishing out what's left of your brain you
so proudly hailed at the twilight's last gleaming.

Let me finish. You missed the service saluting
a breach in the thin blue line, mourning
a friend, a grand, a child.

It is the order of this court that you be taken hence
where a drug cocktail will be administered
and may God shed his grace on thee when all your
appeals are thoroughly dead by a vote of 5 to 4.

It must have been moonglow, way out on the sea,
under a cherry or paper moon tilting toward a destiny,
exceptional and manifest, Clair de Lune and silvery,
living with lunar harmony under the side that shines.

3

The poor children — from smoothly brown and copper
to dark — needed help, some hope, a spark.
But hadn't it always been that way?
The time isn't here — it hasn't arrived —
to lay the white man's burden down near purple
mountains' majesty where we secured
the blessings of our liberty, prosperity —
sorry to those displaced.

Slow moon, heat moon, moon of the big
winds, starting to subside.
The man is in the / dark side of the / bad moon

on the rise.

4

Amid the clatter of drums and the ringing of bells, the
thunderous bass and the flashing of lights, it's party time,
it's bet the house, it's plug in the player names
for the week. It's bitch when the cops say break it up, curse

when the symbols don't line up, retch when you've had your proof
through the night
that your friend is no longer still even quite there,
high on synthetics, meth, heroin, booze . . .

. . . in a moon of forgetting, a moon of sighs, a moon that sparkles
on new fallen snow:

> on the moon river   in a moonshadow
>   on a moondance kind of night
> when the sun has wandered off below,
>   thoroughly moonstruck,
>   thoroughly rolled.

5

This was to be his legacy — a building to carry
his name through time and wipe off
the stain of how it was paid for, how the fortune
behind it was made. For doesn't the preacher always say
when fortune shines, you're in the elect?

Moon of the rockets, moon of red glare.
Moon of the bombs still bursting in air.
Fly me to the rising of the moon some night,

I want to bathe in a rich moonshine
of unalienable rights.

6

Questions got the soldier reading. How did we get here, between
two factions half a world away, who didn't
like us — either one — who didn't want our bombs
bursting in what they prefer to consider their air?
And why were they so willing to die so they could
kill us deep inside a peanut butter-and-jelly
peace spread out on a loaf of prosperity

white which, by the way, has never been equally viewed on
moonbeam / moonshine / moonface nights?
Why were we there and everywhere
where our fathers died?

Lazy moon, thunder moon, moon that once
in a blue moon spits.
Moon of full-moon lunatics, howling.

7

He'd never fired at a person before. He did this time; was
surprised at the groan, at the "Shit! I'm hit!"

Pleased he'd high-fived his gang initiation, his heart pumped hard
all throughout his run-away.
Next day it sank when he learned that he'd killed
an 8-month-old he never even knew was there.

That's another cliche. C'mon, can't you do any better?

Hunting moon, stalking moon; moonless waters
flow by rocks, jutting, split, cut, chopped.

8

The e-mail he opened, surprisingly blunt, should
not have been sent — at least to him. It said that
the cost of the drug they'd bought could be raised
by a thousand or more percent. People pay up
when they land on Park, or on Boardwalk
wearing a big hotel — or when it's paycheck-lender interest
to paycheck-lender rip-off hell
to can't get out from under to not another way.

Flood moon, busting out all over, a raft of silver mouthing
spoons is reaching in your
pocket to promote the general welfare.

9

He administered the cocktail, drug by drug.
There wasn't much twitching — or maybe a lot.
Either way, the end came, the deed was done,
justice established American style (not remotely barbarian
style) in the land of the Pilgrims' pride.

Low moon trudging through the sky,
quaking mostly silently.

10

*There are hardly any good things in this poem — if that's what
it is. This thing is biased, grossly incomplete. Where's the kid*

pulled out of a burning car? First responders helping seniors into boats,
winching them up to safe from harm? The volunteer helping kids to
read? The funds flooding in for storm victims, terror victims, war
victims, more? People trying to cure disease, help the vets, start
a business with decent jobs? Where's feed the hungry,
help the old, shelter the homeless, heal the earth?
So many people helping so many people in so many
wonderful ways — where's a hint of any of that?

Can't say. Don't know. The game's back on.
Don't know. Can't say. I'm brewing tea to contemplate
what I'll buy, where I'll dine, what I'll binge on next
next week. I'm shopping, churching, looking for ways
to decorate. I'm not counting money — that's old-school,
for losers — I'm thoroughly into the art
of the deal, making you go off to hell on your way.
Don't bother me with ethics. It's all about chaos
and cultural war, pay-to-play for more and more.

I'm a man, I have the fun, since all men were
created equal.
I am not: my work is never, ever done.
I'm waiting for the sequel
when well-endowed is not among
the sights we do ordain.

This moves all over the place. Do you know
what the hell you are doing at all?

Moon of red sunsets, moon of fat grass.
Corn moon, berry moon, moon of fatted calves —
will someone weigh it down up there,
walking all around?
Will we hear the clatter, will we hear the sounds?

11

After a short debate, this poem has decided to throw
the following bone to America:

He tossed water and food from the truck. She oversaw
the parachute drop of life-not-death supplies. He
administered many vaccines. She fixed cleft palates, problem
teeth. This was the country of thee I sing, of helping out, of
doing good — the flag still streaming, flag still there — fully the
symbol of all our bling, the stuff they envy, longingly.

It's not very much — but something, I guess.

Moon of long nights, snow moon, freeze —
tough it out as well as you can.
And try to do it gracefully to insure domestic tranquility . . .

when a least-heat moon is pushing
hard to convince a wind it's time to douse the fire that grows
inside the ice, fighting to stay frozen.

12

I am still — supposedly — inside a poem on America. There are
so many rooms in its mansion,
so much on its grounds, so heavy its waters,
that how could I find an end somewhere,
when it seems that alpha has just begun and any omega is only
foreseen, its outline vague if there at all?

America thinks it's ever new, bulldozing much of its ever over.
It's covered by tweets, apps, vaping, uber, fake news, smartphones,
netflix, google,
charter schools, business rules, new and better hacking tools,

craft beers, twitter jeers, sprawling malls with amazon fears.
Drones coming — wait —
they're here; spend another billion for your mercenary team; max
the card out on the latest concert dream. Create the next
investment bubble, go into debt too easily; insist on the pricey
name-brand drug, the one the ads drum on about incessantly and
morbidly, for every trouble, malady,
there's got to be one that works.
Damn the cost, just drop a pill or needle
it in — we need to keep my kin alive; heaven can wait
a little while for grandma, baby, me and mine.

If we don't all learn what we all should know, ignorance
basks in a voting-booth glow
where it's vote my tribe,
no matter who, no matter what they say or do.

That last bit is, at least, so true.

I understand the concept, the reason for America, but
I only vaguely understand why so many still do not.

*Do you really understand? Really? Your negatives say
that you do not. America is optimistic, get it done and
cut the crap. It's pass the chips, let freedom ring,
order out and do it fast, laugh it off, forget the past,
suck it up, latest thing, fix yourself, you're on your own.
(Though I must admit that 'on your own'
isn't quite as true anymore.)*

The moon, perhaps no longer full, is moving into deeper
snow. It drips, runs, pants, hides.
Time to fixate on survive until the next moonrise.

13

She rushed to the phone to make her donation,
gave money she needed to spend on herself for
earthquake / tsunami / tornado relief, to hucksters
selling heavenly briefs they secretly knew were scams.

Too easy. Set up a straw man; knock him down.
Seriously, you can't do any better than this?

Ripening moon. Moon that hides in the high
corn, ready to be plucked.

14

He put on the belt and/or added the horns, then grabbed his
blaster / saber / sword,
smiled at his face, painted for
the con / game / fest / parade or steeled
for a walk down memory lane. It was his patriotic duty to have
some fun and/or be there, saluting, so-cooling over the latest
gaming gun.

After all, his likes would be waiting to welcome him in
and/or the flag would still be there, along with all the cravings
for souvenirs / t-shirts / hats / cards / games plus autographs
and selfies, too,
or pats on the back for a fight well won way back when staying
number one had a price called lots of bombs and guns.
Still does, it seems.

America, you're so damn strong —
can I get a date with you?

Idle moon: some want you to find the dawn,
            some prefer you didn't.

15

This year is it, this year's the one, the future is ours,
it's gotta come. There isn't a place that is better on earth.
I won't hear a word, a phrase against.
You'll jinx it all with your negative vibes. This is the job, the
thing, the one — there can't be any looking back,
no going back, no doubt at all;
it's got to happen the way I want. We're going to win
the goddamn game. It's time to get this
war thing on. Let freedom ring

around the rosy, all fall down in a hip-hop moon,
a rutting moon, a moon that — when the wolves
start in, circling in, leaning in — a howling lunacy
begins, draped in heavy courtroom robes.

16

Pulled up by his own bootstraps, he'd run the thing
for 40 years. Second wife had understood the need for
all the hours. But not the kids — not all, at least —
had crowned his good with brotherhood.

Back to a lot of whining. It's a flip side I can play
as well — but only when I've been out late
and it's almost the dawn's early light.

Moon of frost: shining on a treasure trove
of falling leaves, waiting for a moonquake's heavy
lift to heave a surface open.

17

Visit the city? Why, yes, of course, but wouldn't
consider living there. Too dangerous. Prefer
a slower, know-you pace.
Comfortable in nature's skin — at least more than
you've ever been. Need respect for who we are, what
we do, standing guard.

Moon over clear-cut, stubbled fields,
waving monocrops of grains.
Moon over Currier, moon over Ives,
moon over townscapes losing their shops —
unless the folks with different hues
are asked to enter, settle in.

18

Glad to be needed, needing herself to be out
of the house, it was all about giving to others,
she thought, all about helping smiles
spread out from sea to shining sea.

Another small bone of positive? My spirit soars.
Should my fluttering, stuttering heart
dare hope for just a trifle more?

Moon of charms, tokens, chants.
Moon of distant fonder dreams.

19

First the circle, then the waves; switching colors, thin, then wide.
Letters next, scrawling out. Now
the fine work, signature, the show them what your

paint can do when big is in their face up there —
or hacking interrupts the show.

Spray them. Or hack them. But show them. Doesn't matter
which. Eether, eyether. Other. Both.
Low hanging rusty moon, supermoon, I'm here. Listen. Notice.

20

Why can't we just get something done like they do in, oh,
what's the name of that place?
Not all this goddamn screwin' around, sellin' our souls so
the bleedin' hearts and the real crew of deplorables
can suck at the government's too generous-with-my-money tit?
Not lettin' in losers and danger to stay,
not givin' our sweet land of liberty up
and completely fucking away?

Don't tar us all with what some say.

Moon with trials, melting, heat. Pale moon waits,
then reds, retreats, providing for a common defense.
Moon of hunker down or in, of lock your doors at night from
sin — unless it's been invited in.

21

Again the phrase, not really veiled; again too close; again
the too-long touch or gaze.
The only consolation? There wasn't
a locker room anywhere near, so, no, it wasn't bantering —
though fear followed anger and shame and dismay; they'd
call you a liar, they'd call you a name; you must have
done something, want money or fame,
must have dressed inappropriately. There

isn't another way to explain . . .

> . . . a moon of turnings, returnings, tears,
> a moon of stay on guard for years.

22

A joke abroad in XL wide, a jiggle at home near
mountainsides from sea to warmer rising sea, you pledge
allegiance to the flag, over its singular version
of God, with liberty and justice
for all — written when hope thought a new moon would
rise, keep coming back, renewing the cause.

Moon of the harvest, ripening moon,
please, oh, please, oh, selfie me,
growing wide voluminously where
sugar and syrup will make it show.

23

More than he/she should have skimmed, was pinched, embezzled,
no doubt trimmed.
But the ones who built the grafting tree of intertwined
complexity had walked away, all scot and free,
bounty stuffed inside their pockets, glued to their no-payment
hides; foxes come when hens decide
they just don't need to lock it.

Moon of deliverance, no-stir nights — fat, full moon, stay
fat tonight.

24

The signs are on the streets again, dueling in spins, competing for
sends that say go forth
and trend and trend and while you're at it, get out
of my way, I'm flying where it's warm today,
where I hope no one can spy on me. The family needs a break
from things, from all the stress I lay on them.

It's more than just pursuit, you know. We deserve to be happy —
it's one of our rights.
It's in the founding document;
it's there in black, it's there in white.

I notice there's no Creator here. You'll never win friends, influence
people or make the top,
with a less than is dreamed of, can't be a winner, stuck as a loser
philosophy shit.

Moons wait for suns to dip in their toes —
fiery toes way out on the sea — hesitantly.

25

Moon of the Moby-white Dick on display wants Daddy
to make it all better, OK?
No matter the cost, no matter the price.
Just help us, please, we'll roll the dice.
More people doin' well in the world? Makes us peak-ed, jealous,
gray; that's not what
we actually really want. And though the globe may be
running hotter, not everyone's ready to check on its
fever above the (are they?) fruited plains that try
to keep the weeds away while bees, just trying to pollinate,
are collateral damage losing their way
whether it's to or whether it's from . . .

. . . the thunder moon, the envy moon,
  the moon of settling scores.

26

And speaking of scores, can you check on mine?
Do you have a fact that matches with mine,
when cables (seen snapping both here and there)
show raining and sun at the very same time?

That's it; please quit — I say you are more than done.
Very unbalanced, most wearisome. Dour, gloomy,
way incomplete, poorly constructed and very unfair
on a way too negative balance sheet.

True, true, very true, but good doesn't make up most of
the news. Here, perhaps, is something that you may come
to appreciate just a bit more:

Waxing, waning, moon of mine, accept my mea culpa, shine,
on my so trite apology.
This was supposed to be poetry, but it doesn't matter much if it's
not because nobody reads the stuff anymore —
not enough of the people who count.
Our culture is movies with action and gore,
Disney and Lucas and give me some more
reality shows with lots of fake boobs
and combover hair not a joke anymore.

Moon in a series of duels with the sun,
does moonstone shine when it's cooked just a bit
or must it be charred and quite, quite done?

27

This poem may have a limit, it seems, but it
cannot have an end.

America poems have a destiny, must spin around in more
repeats, looking for eyeballs out
on the streets even when winter is raging and tweets and
ads are a part of the wasteland sleet —
the American dream has serious boundary issues.

Frost moon, frozen moon, going round and ever round
and ever round again, pulling slowly off,
away from an earth from whence it came —
the moonlight sonata / serenade is playing the notes for
the faithful today and will play them for every America
day that's still to dawn, that's still to come,
that still has time to rise and run.

I am in love with what could
become a place we call
America.

Final Movement:
Mostly Darker Notes

empty lesson

the taste of matches,
used, discarded.

a line of sight,
smoky, ashen.

a glow of rooms,
disregarded.

tender-stepping
cats, kisses out
of reach,

a burn
that will
not understand,

that does not
want to talk

or teach.

A Modest List of Indescribable

Black holes. Space. The universe.
The brief perfume
of turpentine.
Licking off a mixer blade.
Sudden leaves that rasp on stone.
Black dirt giving in
to deeply urgent spade.

A horn leading echoes
from a brassy hiding-out.
A waterfall.
A fire cradling its wood.
A pet of fur. A panting dog.
A wheel-around of late-night doubt.
A catch of cedar-scented burn.

Curves. Sex.
Rhythm forcing cautious feet.
Bodies blind to their ease of leap.
The sounding off of wind in taller
yearning trees.
An idling motor's hum.
A wasp of incense smoking
in a burner, risingly. Scissors slicing
paper, carving card stock out.
A car door's clinching, seizing thump.
A sliding key, turning in;
the bolt of a satisfied lock.
Smooth skin — warm.
Knowing what elation is
while it's wearing thin.
A slide guitar's finishing note.
Smooth metal, wood, stone.

Sneezes.
Just-baked bread.

Just-mown grass.
A spider web.
The last bite, last spoon —
not enough, comes too soon.

Just blue.
Just green.
A freshly spiraled orange peel.

Coffee your way, morning, news.
Lilacs in the dooryard bloomed.
The almost word.
Trying to explain why
something's absurd.

Surprises flattering retinas,
puzzles stuttering brains.
The exult of a distant crowd.
The smell of after-rain.

The tyranny of when and how.
The disappearing
sound of trains.

Old-Fashioned

I cry not scalding tears
but I sing my lamentations unto thee.

I wrote like that in early poems.
Today throws brickbats at such language:
pretentious, outdated, old-fashioned, passé.

I always thought such phrases held a power.
I will go to my grave still thinking they do.

We lose something when we choose
to mount what our forebears forged
under glass marked "Please, Don't Touch."
We are the worse when we do not roll on
mighty waters, when we do not drip
our pens from the river of blood that time
has wrought, when we do not ride
the cataracts that fall to us in floods
and waves of crosscut screams
and whispered shouts to shake
us from an indolent sleep or a doleful,
labored, fitful rest.

Perhaps the future will treasure
old-fashioned more than we do,
will look back on our linguistic restraints
as quaint, provincial, narrow, misguided.

If so, I will be able to say unto them:

Abandon all your forms of wrath,
and cry not scalding tears.

The Dominion of Rats

The dominion of rats emerges and swarms
as if it were a living thing, as if it had
weight or mattered. Rats scatter,
then hustle by leaps and tumble by bounds, trying
to escape a drowning ground, trying not to fumble
after leaping away from the tinny sounds that resemble
laughs, that want to keep time and juggle rings,
use razors to force a line to sing and pull on jagged
cantilevered strings, where puppets
don't know what's going on.
When it's not too hot and not too cold, the clock chimes,
the rhyme turns and the rats all
scramble for cover, hover in lines away from the front,
parallel, facing, still in the hunt.

Fire. Tools. Cave paint. Rules.
Roaring jets and finishing schools.
But sweet lovers run afoul of tribes that stand
stock still, who proudly deny and reprimand
what will not rhyme with orthodox, what will not wear
what's properly worn or shout enough of shrill.
The tribes shield all their sins within.
Their tinny sounds, which should not matter,
clatter on, making shatter from upside-down
as a holy summing-up begins.

The rats, betting big and making chatter,
and thinking still that somehow, some way,
they still matter — decide it's best to take the bait,
to risk their accidental fate and time their hymn
and speak their ever-growing patter
when they think that there's the slightest chance
that they can win, can climb the hill, that they might
sometime somewhere somehow maybe
someday matter still . . .

. . . even though the cold
grows dark and the day
decides it must stand down,
even though the wind rains
blows that squint in streaks,
and even though the silence,
growing ever starker,
sits upon a voiceless hill,
ever   only   always   still.

Guilt

I am the lead-on
for the teams
of horses
walking onto
the field
of stars, prancing
where the no

earth falls.

Eyes that look up,
pleadingly,
sweating
in a desert
whose ironic name
they'll never know,

can't eat stars,
don't know prance,

won't learn shame.

Dogs Barking a Language at Night

A dog barks two doors down,
then next door, then up the street.
Are they speaking a language
we don't understand?

I move through stars, not even a singe.

Money hauls its various selves
to its various homes.
It used to be sheepish — it's learned.

Rejoice needs a reason now.
(Maybe if flags were not aloft,
dropping bombs on the weak and soft?)

Mercy? Still losing its appeals.

Time's headache just won't stop,
even with all the pills it takes.

If a miracle happens to walk down
the street, I won't mind if you
shake me awake.

The dogs are quiet.
Language has taken a longingly break.

Force tops love, death checkmate.

Shoveling Snow

The snow has had its
chances to turn itself to ice —
they weren't wasted.

Trains groan over cold rails.
Hustling trucks slide into stops.
Houses quietly puff our future
into absorbent skies
that grab every bit of gray
they can.

I pause from shoveling snow —
to listen to the sound of
one small dog
barking at the universe.

The Stars, Unmasked

The stars are:

    fireflies, stilled;

    birds, mostly white, perched until
      until arrives;

    lanterns peeking out from caves;

    bits of sprinkled salt, saved;

    thoughts pushed out a strainer
      from another universe;

    left-overs after birds stopped
      pecking through a heavenly veil;

    shimmer — because we won't stand still,
      don't like stillness much at all;

    all the tears that will ever fall
      and they're all right there for all to see.

Mattering

Bullets prowl the hang-out streets,
ricochet their hitting home,
rooting into bodies and the body politic
until fear stalks the polls and leaves
the ruins out like trash for night to find.

But night makes a choice —
it steps over, won't raise an alarm —
it's dawn's job to pick up sticks,
to do all the real throwing away,
pay all the real never mind.

What I want to know is this:
Is it just like this
out on the galactic rim?
Hell, even much closer than that.
Is it like this on a planet orbiting
the stars that are just next door,
the ones — at 36K miles per hour —
only 78,000 years away?

Do they do it any better there?
That's what I want to know.
And if and when they give up hope,
throw in their galactic towel, will it
matter anywhere, anywhere else at all?

Take Blue

Take blue — please.
Go ahead, it's good for you.
Uncorked, breathing, brackish, dark,
poured on your days along with your nights.
Pour till it's mop-it-up, cup-runneth-over
long past closing time.

Take red. Supposedly hot,
fire, coals — but all this time it's just pretend.
Red needs to fake it because it's afraid,
afraid you won't let it in when you learn
that it plans to dissolve in crumples and tears,
to shake its snotty spit around
and wipe it off on all your chairs.

Take green. Who wouldn't?
Growth, new, spring, life — but is that a cover
for worn-out seeds, or what you could barely
call worry beads that it fingered so long beneath
a veneer that they're no longer up to the job?

Take silver — all 30 pieces,
I believe. Let their shiny hypnotize, even when
every breeze describes that all they are is gray
unless some light's around to tease.

Take gold. You know you want to, can't
resist. It's Croesus counting coins, sunshine
selling speculate. It's all the universe needs a break,
awaits permission to come ashore for party time,
relieve the bore. Gold does a lot of aspirin,
but its pain remains out and about,
lost in a lot of muttering, left and right and flank.

Take black. Half a month can
disappear in less than half a day; half a year in just

a week, maybe even less. There's no escaping
through a name, no sliding through
a narrow space. You're stuck inside, it's panic
time, you chose the losing race.

Take white. Try to answer the question mark
it left upon the land. Be sure to hollow
a space for it — even your best chair may not do.
Be sure to send a thank you note
when it cuts another frilly piece for one
more bloody wedding gown.

Take blue — again.
Blisters may want you to amputate, but
blue is good, still good for you, even when
Joe and a quarter-to-three are ready
and waiting to serve, one stiff drink already poured,
stronger than any wine you know —
or ever will.

Take blue — and please try not to spill.

Mapmaker

The mapmaker blinked — a street
was gone. Shavings of lead, planed away
by an inadvertent forearm
blade, were curling off a wary
map, alone, distressed, afraid.

The mapmaker yawned
and stretched and yawned —
a city went missing, a county was lost,
a stream would drip dry before dawn.

The mapmaker shrugged, rose, turned —
had done what any rocket could do.
Blotting out history, making inconvenient truths
into packets convenient enough to discard —
just a good day's work, or so he thought,
not all that terribly hard.

What's all this fuss about excising history?
he asked himself when he took a break.
An erasure here, a coffee spill there,
a line through a name so it didn't appear
on a subsequent map — that's all it took.
Oh, well, he thought, *I guess I'll never
understand why they get so overly exercised
about something so easy to do.*

He yawned again. It was time for a nap,
though he thought he might tuck with a book
before that. The rest could wait till tomorrow.
No one would listen for tiny cries.
And if anyone happened to hear,
those cries would be ignored.
The instructions couldn't be misconstrued —

they were very cut and very dried.

Strangers Passed on a Walk to the Store

There was a toddler in a stroller who turned
her head to follow me as long as she could.
There was a college kid with rainbow hair,
his head glued on a sightline rope
to a small screen fixed at the end of his arms.
He didn't unglue a single eye when our paths
briefly crossed. There was a 40-something

jogger willing to risk a fall on the ice so he
didn't have to break his stride. And there was
a woman, well into her 60s and far into losing
her battle with weight. The nods we exchanged
might have been code for: *Thank heaven —
who thought we would make it this far?*

But, to be honest, I have to admit that I only
remembered any of them because I thought they
were needed to flesh out a poem — this poem.

The real poem starts right here with two "bookends":
a thin young girl tussling with a family dog,
and a very old woman, bent and curled, cane in hand,
her slow-motion steps latching tight to

iffy ground. When I asked if the dog was tough
to hold, (it was working hard to dive in the street),
the girl suddenly flashed a grin that only kids who
live in safe can ever smile, then flashed it again
as she walked by, arm pulled taut by her
let's-go dog. It was the kind of smile you bask in,
take back home for a sit by a fire — before age
begins a tempering, a pick-at-it, toughen-it,
cover-it-up, a drive-it-to-under, stretch-it-to-thin.
The old woman, who could only manage

a quick look-up to see who was there as I
walked by, was no doubt concerned about taking
a fall, knowing what it can mean when you're
already crawling in sight of your home.
But despite all that, or maybe because, a hint of
a smile just might have been there —

part summing-up; part yes, I recall;
part where-did-it-go? part damn, I'm not through —

before her attention was needed elsewhere
for the critical task at hand.

She

She would slice
the talk up into strips,
broil them in fat
(if she could),
race the wind of her
fidgety youth right out
of here and do it all
— all of it —
righteous good.

Instead it's dead
of stare and look.
Instead it's wait
for the real thing
to undertake
a final move
heading west or south.

She would be a danger,
covered in some
chitin spikes,
if there was any energy
to move a lever,
flap a wing.

Chess Match

The sighing of winds.

The baying of wolves.

The holy of cups, sliced by hooves,
patched by prayer, reborn.

A maneuver of troops.

A like of likes, forgiven.

The move that's mostly forbidden.

A grind of lathes.

A slash of sins.

A tribe of lights made out of fire.

A ripple of sinister winds.

A sorrow of diamonds, ridden hard, put up wet.

Snowy moons; pure stealth.

The deep earth, slanting in to some of its dreams.

A rare tithe of sharp hooks.

A loop tied, a simple song.

Rook takes pawn, forgets its place.

A bandit escapes, the queen rants.

Knight takes toll, then recants.

Castles crash straight on through.

The fool's lament is overdue.

The heart blooms, carmine red.

The tailor's needle, deft, true, pokes
the thread quickly through.

A hope runs off, one wrong way,
says a prayer, is brought to bay.

The spit turns. Make the move.
Checkmate. The king is dead.

Perhaps the triangle

Perhaps the triangle
lived inside the first hot
dot of everything, in the first
hot spot that incredibly
banged; perhaps its form
was needed, inherent, ready
to step in the frame.

Perhaps the shape of a tree
or a hand or a sail was there —
in potential, waiting,
all part of a coiled spring
in no hurry to unwind.

Perhaps the virus, pain, death,
as well as so much suffering,
were all imagined, predicted,
foreshadowed, sitting
there outside of time,
waiting to be born.

Perhaps my eyes or your eyes
winked once inside
a gathering cloud of gaseous
dark and floating
dust, ready to ignite.

Perhaps we were foretold,
perhaps we were intended.

Perhaps the accidental
light that salts our only
universe, that forms
clusters and eddies
and strings so large
our brains ache

trying to grasp them,
perhaps all of it was
once a dream
where every blinding
bluest sky was softened
by a perfect wind
that we were never
meant to know.

Cycle

I congealed from stars
where weeping was not allowed,
where valleys could not cry
out to their sisters, call
out to their brothers.
Dropped, mute, into a celluloid
dream, I was weaned,
quickly, taught, weakly,
dried with a trite blond glaze.

The prophets were not blind —
they were not yet even born.
The tale, told by an idiot, was
not yet written or even conceived.
The sun, tired of sweeping out
great magnetic curves,
directed its repeating drum
elsewhere, pushed its music on
ears not yet designed to hear.

It is obvious. I am sad.
The sunset was breathtaking,
the starshine exhilarating,
but the slow goodbye is tedious,
the timbre and tone repetitive,
unglamorous, regrettable.

In the night, past sleep, past
knowing, screens tick words,
pictures pulse, morning is
blocked, turning any
conceivable message
into reams of meaningless,
markings of uselessness.

The road is pitted and rough,
has knots and convolutions,
ribbons and parabolas,
confusion and paranoia.

I stumble up the last stairs.
I put out the last light.
I have come around, again.
I am spinning with gasses,
hurtling with rocks, smashing
and gnashing my teeth, again.
I am writhing, seeping,
soaring, creeping.
I am weeds and pods, clods
and barbs, planted and seeding,
again and again.
I am some kind of nautilus,
darting again, chambered again,
ancient and unplumbed,
newborn, neutral, naked, numb,
still with eyes that want to burn,
still too wet behind some ears
that hear too many drums.

I have come around, again,
from melody and prosody,
from energy and anarchy,
from blasphemy and monotony;
I have come around, again,
and it is all buried in a golden
spiral that is but does not know.
I have come around, again,
congealed, again,
from smoke, from dross,
from hope, from loss —

from stars, crossed,
and filled with

exploding nails.

Acknowledgments

Very special thanks to my wife, Bonnie, to my children Matthew and Laura, and to my "adopted" children Yannan Hu and Danny George. I'd also like to thank the members of my writers group — Carrie Bassett, Stephanie Brown, Kathleen Kimball-Baker and Susan Spindler — for their help and encouragement. Ethna McKiernan, Kevin FitzPatrick, Dave Moore and Frank Hudson also deserve my thanks for their helpful critiques over the years. And, lastly, my thanks go to S. R. Stewart, Rubie Grayson and the dedicated people at Unsolicited Press for making this book possible.

A few of the poems in this collection appeared in the following publications: *Conclave, Jenny, the Minnesota Daily, Pinyon Review, A quiet courage, Red Paint Hill Poetry Journal, Route 7 Review* and *Third Wednesday.* Poems also appeared in the chapbooks *Thresholds* and *Living Here: Poems About Neighborhoods.*

Notes

To the Reader: Many poems in this collection are dark. But though I admit to being a pessimist, I'm neither depressed nor unhappy (except about growing older). Perhaps that's because the poems are a kind of therapy, "sucking out some venom."

The Locusts. Contains phrases from poems by Sylvia Plath.

Rowing for Real. This poem references Anne Sexton's *The Awful Rowing Toward God.*

Love Poem. The first line is also the first line of a poem by e. e. cummings.

Cycle. Stars fuse hydrogen atoms to create energy. When a star runs out of these atoms, it starts using the helium atoms that the fusion process created. As these atoms are depleted, the fusion process creates and uses the atoms of heavier and heavier elements. Once the star creates iron atoms, however, the fusion process stops. Gravity collapses the star and, almost instantaneously, it explodes, with much of its matter blown into space. This includes the iron in our blood, the iron that makes up most of the earth's molten core and, of course, the iron found in many nails.

About the Author

Jim Bohen is a poet and songwriter who was born and raised in St. Paul, Minnesota, where he currently lives with his wife, Bonnie. A graduate of the (then) College of St. Thomas, he's worked for non-profits and a book publisher, been the lead singer in rock and acoustic groups, and spent the last 25 years as a freelance writer/editor. His poems have appeared in *Conclave, the Minnesota Daily, Red Paint Hill, Third Wednesday* and elsewhere. He's been shortlisted for the erbacce prize and a finalist for The Loft Literary Center's Mentor Series. *I travel in rusting burned-out sedans* is his first book. A prolific songwriter, his CD, *Never Too Late*, features 12 of the hundreds of songs he's written. (Samples can be heard at iTunes and cdbaby; search for "J B and the Phantom Band.") More can be learned at http://jimbohen.weebly.com.

About the Press

Unsolicited Press is a small press in the Pacific Northwest that is operated by a team of volunteers. The team works to publish stellar poetry, fiction, and creative nonfiction. Learn more at www.unsolicitedpress.com.

CPSIA information can be obtained
at www.ICGtesting.com
Printed in the USA
FFHW021958031219
56536452-62384FF